Reflections From The Porch

Life Lessons from Boggy Road

Also by
Jean B. Burden

Reflections From the Parlor:
A Pilgrim's Spiritual Journey

Reflections From the Pond:
Constant Faith From a New View

All of Jean's works can be purchased online at Amazon, Barnes & Noble and most other online bookstores. They can also be found at Papa's General Store in Conway, South Carolina.

Reflections From the Porch

Life Lessons from Boggy Road

Jean B. Burden

TEL Publishing

For further information from Jean B. Burden regarding her availability for worship conferences or speaking events, please contact Jean at lilymom7@gmail.com

Copyright ©2018 by Jean B. Burden

Cover Design: Stephen Lursen Art

Cover Photography: Jean Burden

Publisher: TEL Publishing, Charlotte, NC

ISBN: 978-1-970094-00-8

All rights reserved. No part of this publication may be reproduced, stored in a retrieval system or transmitted in any form or by any means, electronic, digital, mechanical, photocopying, recording, or otherwise, without the prior written permission of the copyright owner.

Unless otherwise noted, all Scripture quotations are taken from the Christian Standard Bible®, Copyright © 2017 by Holman Bible Publishers. Used by permission. Christian Standard Bible® and CSB® are federally registered trademarks of Holman Bible Publishers.

Scripture quotations marked (NIV) are taken from the Holy Bible, New International Version®, NIV®. Copyright © 1973, 1978, 1984, 2011 by Biblica, Inc.™ Used by permission of Zondervan. All rights reserved worldwide. www.zondervan.com The "NIV" and "New International Version" are trademarks registered in the United States Patent and Trademark Office by Biblica, Inc.™

Library of Congress Cataloging-in-Publication Data

Burden, Jean B., 1957-

reflections from the porch: life lessons from boggy road

Library of Congress Control Number: 2018964649

Dedication

To the women in my home Bible study. We have learned together, loved together, cried together, laughed together, and most of all, grown together in God's Word. I cherish every minute with you.

Contents

Introduction	9
1 – It's All About Position	12
2 – Stop the Grumbling!	17
3 – They Should Have Been Safe	22
4 – Jake and the Bully	26
5 – A Frog in My Path	30
6 – A Full House	34
7 – A Journey of Faith	37
8 – A New Month . . . and It's War	40
9 – Awed By Creation	44
10 – Bloom When It's Time	48
11 – Choosing a Door	52
12 – Comfort Foods and Such	55
13 – Damaged and Beautiful	57
14 – Going Back Is Hard!	62
15 – Good Friday Thankfulness	66
16 – A Grandmother's Dreams	68
17 – He's Everywhere	72
18 – Hula Hoop Prayer	77
19 – Not Naturally Equipped	80
20 – Living with a "Fixer"	82
21 – Missing the Truths	85
22 – Okay? Stop Asking and Be Decisive!	90
23 – Who's Your Daddy?	93
24 – Just An Ordinary Little Girl	96
25 – Top Ten for Today	100

26 – When Life Gets Top-Heavy	103
27 – The World's Confusion	107
28 – He Was a Good, Good Father	111
29 – Thanking the Saints	118
30 – Weeds: A Never-ending Reality	121
31 – Finding Faith in the Storm	125
32 – Waiting for the Other Shoe to Drop	129
33 – Preparation Meets Faith	133
34 – Lessons from Another Valley	137
35 - Trapped	140
36 – Putting Out the Welcome Mat	145
37 – Don't Move the Barricade!	149
38 – More Lessons from Yoga	152
39 – The Paradox of the Old and the New	156
40 – God's "Omni" Is Everything We Need	159
An Addendum: Prayer for Teachers and Children	163
Works Cited	167

Introduction

It's been two years since the release of my last book, *Reflections from the Pond,* and a lot has changed during this time. After much prayer, I felt led to leave the music ministry for a while, returning to church with my husband in Conway, South Carolina. For the first few months, as much as I love to sing, I wouldn't even sing in the choir --- I just wanted to sit on the pew, soak in some Bible teaching, and worship with abandon. It was a great decision, and even after I joined the choir and praise team again, I loved returning to the pew to sit with my husband as our pastor delivered a true teaching of God's word week after week. So this book is filled with reflections from the pew because that's where my time has been spent for the last two years. The other place in which I've spent the bulk of my time is on Boggy Road, the location of our family "compound." Some of my best prayer time is spent in a rocking chair on my wrap-around porch, where I can see and be overwhelmed by the bounty of God's creation.

Other things in my life have changed as well. After spending four years as a teacher recruiter in South Carolina, I retired from full-time work (for the second time!) in June, 2018. God clearly directed that decision because He had other plans for me in this season. I am teaching part-time in the middle level education programs at Coastal Carolina

Jean B. Burden

University and Horry-Georgetown Tech, and every day feels like a mission field as I listen, love and share with young people who enter my door. I love to affect the way they view the urgent task of loving God's children in public schools and the way they approach their calling as teachers. Every missionary doesn't have to work for the church, and teaching continues to be a mission field.

Last summer we turned a lifelong hobby into a reality by opening Grandma's Legacy Lilies, a daylily farm, on our property. The work was hard, and Hurricane Florence took a toll on our little farm, but next year will be easier, and the beauty of God's flowers never ceases to amaze me. The daylilies have opened the door for new friends, and I have had a chance to share my love of flowers with others. I love knowing that my flowers are making another person's space more beautiful!

I tell you all of this to say one thing: every season of life brings changes, but with each change, God has a clear plan. I have practiced stepping into the waves and learning to take His hand, even when I cannot see the exact path He has chosen for me. My faith has grown as I have walked through some dark valleys with Him, knowing He would never leave me there. I bring you this book today as a woman who loves Him even more and wants nothing more than to be in His service --- however and whenever He sees fit! Having reached the beautiful age of 60, I realize that I don't want to miss a thing He has in store!

Join me as I share my *Reflections from the Porch: Life Lessons from Boggy Road.*

Blessings and love,

JeanB

It's All About Position

In real estate we hear, "Location, location, location." In my college work with pre-service teachers, I declare over and over, "Relationships, relationships, relationships." Both of these words --- location and relationship --- impact our walk with God, but even more than these, what matters is, "Position, position, position." We must position ourselves to hear from God, walk in His will, and stand firm against Satan and sin.

Think about a football field full of players. What is it that determines where each player places himself in the play to have the most impact toward success? Position. Think about the police on a raid. What determines how they quietly sneak into a situation, creating a surprise attack? Position. Think about your relationship with God. What is it that determines the depth and width and strength of that relationship? Position. Let me explain.

I have been reading a wonderful book by Anne Graham Lotz: *The Daniel Key.* In this short but powerful text she says that, like Daniel in the Old Testament, we must create a daily rhythm of study and prayer. But to do that, I believe we must position ourselves to pray and study God's word, writing its truths on our hearts so they become a part of us. Positioning ourselves to study His Word and hear His voice means we must make choices of position: we must position ourselves in our daily schedule to place Him first. We must position ourselves in a physical location where we can study and pray without worldly interruptions. We must position our hearts to lean on His understanding of the Word and to hear His voice. It's all about position.

In yoga we do a pose called Mountain Pose. It involves standing with all of my weight on one leg, while placing the other foot either against my ankle, my calf, or my thigh. But that's just the first step. Next I must tighten my body and pull it up toward the sky, using my muscles to create a tall tower. Then I place my hands in prayer mode and lift them to the sky, all the while finding a spot on which to focus my eyes so I am not distracted by anything that would steal my power and balance. In this position I can stand strong, and my instructor, Emily, tells us to be so strong that nothing can knock us down. Mountain pose is a good metaphor for positioning ourselves with God.

Think about it like this: we stand tall in His strength, pulling our hearts and minds toward Him, and lifting our prayers to the heavens, just like I lift my hands in the pose. Then we must find our focus --- God, and God alone --- so nothing can take our eyes off God, our Father, and Jesus, our Savior. When I place myself in this pose and put on His armor, nothing can knock me down in life . . . ***nothing***. Oh, yes, Satan can try to pull you and me away from God with flaming arrows of doubt, distraction, worry, fear . . . whatever tool he believes will take our hearts and minds off God so he can "knock us over" into defeat and despair. And we can be stubbornly willful, taking ourselves out of God's plan for our lives. But we don't have to allow this. We can position ourselves in a mountain pose of God's Word, knowing that our most urgent focus must be our adoption as His children and our relationship with Him . . . the One for whom nothing is impossible.

When I started yoga, I couldn't stand firm for even a few seconds. I was wobbling and struggling, and in fact, I would stand close enough to the wall that I could catch myself when I fell. Some days were better than others, but I fell for a very long time. But now? I rarely fall because I have learned that the secret is tightening my core and pulling myself up with core strength. This is true in life as well. As we begin to position ourselves to hear from God and commit His word to our hearts and minds, we will wobble some days. Satan will convince us that we don't have time or we need to start our to-do list, or he will even attempt to convince us that our time "in position" with God is not urgent. I can almost hear him saying, "Do it later; it will wait." But remember: he is a liar and a thief, and he comes with a singular purpose: to kill, steal and destroy everything that would keep us close to our Father and positioned in His strength.

We can't let Satan knock us over or push us out of position.

So let's get practical for a moment. How do we position ourselves in this crazy, noisy world? First, we must create a space where we can spend time with God. Did you see the movie "War Room"? She used her closet to position herself with God and His Word, even taping scriptures to the walls. Creating a space is urgent because it cuts the noise and sets us apart to be with our Father. Second, we must set an appointment with God every single day. The space is useless if we don't go there and seek Him, His Word, and His Will. We must make a choice to keep our appointments with Him so we are positioned to seek understanding and discernment of His Word in our lives. Third, we need to make adjustments in our daily walk so we are positioned to pray without ceasing throughout the day and to feel the nudging of the Holy Spirit. For me this first involved switching my radio station to K-Love. It sent me to work with songs of praise on my heart, and I found myself singing them all day. When my children were not in the car, I positioned myself by listening to Christian study books on CD. Both of these helped me to position my heart to stand tall with God all day, not just during my quiet time with Him in the morning. These simple choices positioned me to become stronger and more in love with God's Word.

One last thought: life is going to throw us incredible disappointments, challenges, and heartaches. By choosing Godly position in advance of these difficult times, we don't have to fall and crumble to the ground in response to the curve balls of life. Jesus told us life would be hard, but He also told us to rejoice because He is our Overcomer. I have faced a whole lot of difficulty and devastating events in 2018, some of which you will read in this book, and even yesterday Satan wanted me to believe that I am not strong enough to be the woman God has called me to be. But this morning, I positioned myself in God's Word, seeking scriptures that address the very things that were burdening my heart. Then I took those Words of God and prayed them back to Him, prophesying victory in every situation. I positioned myself for victory; it was a choice, not an accident, and as I write today, I know I am standing in a mountain pose of God's might. After all, He is the God of the impossible! We don't serve a wimp; we serve a mighty Warrior! In the words of a favorite song: "Savior . . . He can move the mountains. Our God is mighty to save; He is mighty to save. Forever, author of salvation; He rose and conquered the grave; Jesus conquered the grave."

No small feat . . . He overcame death, and as we position ourselves with God, we can overcome anything that life and Satan throw our way. I am standing in mountain pose this morning as living proof of God's goodness in the land of the living. I pray you will position yourself to stand in victory with Him, too!

Stop the Grumbling!

Philippians 2:14 says this: "Do everything without grumbling or arguing." Another version uses the words "without complaining." This verse was an eye-opener for me a number of years ago because I could always find myself in a place of grumbling when life would dish out some junk or I threw myself into a mess with poor choices. Grumbling in the teachers' lounge at school. Grumbling about things that went wrong at home. Grumbling about . . . well, you know, just about anything.

But then this verse crossed my path and changed my thinking and my heart. And so, there's a lesson to be learned, but I need to share a story.

Last week I listened to a wonderful Dave Ramsey video in which he reminded us to prepare for emergencies. Why? Because they WILL come. No doubt about it. Well, this week in my world hasn't been about financial emergencies but about life's minor inconveniences and major tragedies, and I've had to hear Philippians 2:14 in my head all week. I want to share so maybe, if you are a complainer, you can get a fresh perspective on the attitude God expects.

Monday morning was beautiful, and I was looking forward to some down time after two very busy weeks and weekends in a row. But at 9:30 AM, I received news that our niece's husband had died unexpectedly. It changed the whole course of her life, and in mundane ways, it changed the whole course of our week. But instead of complaining (my old habit), I found myself being grateful that we live close enough to be there for the family. We were able to visit and love, and I was able to give to her through my gift of music. It was such a privilege to use God's gift in me, worshiping through playing the piano, to honor Michael's life. I sang at their wedding, and I played with my heart at his going-home celebration. We will continue to be grieved over Michael's death, but we celebrate his place in heaven and the legacy he left behind.

And then Tuesday came. I took my car to have the tires checked because the tires were losing air. I thought they would "patch" a leak, but no: I had to replace two tires unexpectedly. That sweet man at Martin's Tire said, "I'm so sorry. This is going to cost you a lot." My response, instead of complaining became, "It's okay. You are going to keep me safe as we travel this week to be with family, and I'm grateful." But the day wasn't over yet. I won't even explain, but in trying to be helpful to someone else, I suffered some deep puncture wounds from a cat. This caused me some concern because I've had major problems from a cat-situation before, and my spirit wanted to complain and be fearful. But instead, I listened to my friends (thank you, friends!), gave up my Wednesday morning to go to the doctor, and I received antibiotics to ward off bacterial infection. By the time I finished at the doctor and the pharmacy, my morning was shot, but instead of complaining, I found myself grateful for the peace that came with good medical care and the joy of having good insurance. And the week was only halfway through.

Thursday morning . . . headed to gym and work, but I got rerouted in a hurry, because one of my dearest friends, Marie LaValle Nuckles, was in a serious car accident. Complain about loss of time? No way. Grateful that God put me in town so I could get to her quickly? Oh, you better believe it. She lives in Georgetown but they took her to Conway Hospital. I knew it had to be a God-appointment, and I showed up.

Friday brought its own share of bumps in the road, but here's the point: I live in a place with God that I can now thank Him, not FOR the difficulties, but IN the difficulties. I can have a grateful heart even when things are challenging. Years ago, I failed in this area over and over, and even when I learned not to complain out loud, I still let a lot of grumbling run through my head. But no more. How did that happen? First, I had to repent, and then I had to practice over and over and over and over, allowing the Holy Spirit to guide my heart and my words. Through God's Word I learned to re-train my mind, heart and mouth to think and say the positives, not the negatives . . . to focus on the good, not the bad. I had to, as Scripture says, hide God's Word in my heart so I won't sin against Him, and one of His Words that I hid in my heart was the scripture about not complaining about anything. Not traffic, not sickness, not accidents, not daily aggravations . . . not anything. So how does God expect this of us?

God is an omnipresent God, always here with us and for us in every situation. Everything that happens to us is not good, but God is always near, waiting to comfort, sustain, and love. When we choose to think differently and seek Him, He can take the worst of situations and make something good come from it. In the words of James Bryan Smith (*The Good and Beautiful God*) we must practice "soul training," which means practicing the spiritual disciplines God gave us: prayer and study (and there are others). These are vital because they lead us to greater faith, a renewed mind through His Word, a different attitude toward life, a changed heart . . . things that seem difficult and even impossible, but nothing is impossible when we walk with and trust God, our Father.

This story is *not* a narrative of bragging about me; it's a story of a mess of a life, redeemed by a Savior who died to save me, a Father who has adored me since before I was formed in the womb and adores me still, and a Holy Spirit living within me, nudging me to change and grow and become more like the woman God designed me to be. He didn't design me to be a negative complainer; He designed all of us to walk in His ways, love Him first and most, and glorify Him with our actions. Maybe like me, your earthly daddy told you something like this: "When you go places, tell them who your daddy is, and make me proud." I want to go everywhere and do everything with that in mind: I want to tell everyone, with my words and my actions, who my Daddy is, and I want to make Him proud. Being a complainer simply doesn't honor the God I serve and love.

Today I encourage you to write Philippians 2:14 on your heart. Practice some soul training so you can change old habits into new ones. With every situation, refuse to allow your mind to go down the negative rabbit hole, but instead, choose to cling to God and ask the Holy Spirit to guide you to a changed and renewed mind. Will things still be painful and difficult? Yes, Jesus Himself said that this world is full of trials and tribulations, but that's not the end of the verse. He said that we must "take heart" because He has overcome this world, and when we choose Jesus, giving Him first place in our lives, minds, and hearts, we become overcomers right alongside Him. Amazing? Oh, yes, but so completely true. Be a victor today by allowing Him to transform your heart and mind so you will walk worthy of your calling as His sons and daughters.

Jean B. Burden

They Should Have Been Safe

We live on almost sixty-five acres in the country. We are surrounded by woods and ponds, and there is more room to run that we can ever use. This is a paradise for explorers and a haven of peace. When we moved out here in 2015, it gave me so much joy to give my two labs, Belle and Eliza, a safe place to run and live. Even before we moved, we would bring them out here to spend a day, and their joy abounded! They ran, sniffed, explored, and played. When they got too hot, they went for a swim, and when they were tired, they napped under a tree. It is dog perfection, or at least we thought. In 2017, we buried our second dog in a five month span, and as I sit here, the thought keeps ringing through my head, "They should have been safe. They should have been safe. They should have been safe."

You might say that our little farm puts us in a bubble --- a bubble of protection from the real world, but the truth is that the real world is out there, just beyond our property, on Highway 22. We believe that Eliza and Red, her puppy, followed their friend, Brownie, onto the highway, and this is not an easy feat. In fact, getting there is quite complicated, unless you are following someone who is leading you to destruction. I'm sure he didn't mean to hurt them, but in following him and not being savvy about highways and other such dangers, they are gone. Both of them died a horrific death, and our bubble has been broken. And this reminds me of an urgent spiritual truth.

Satan and his emissaries sneak into our bubbles, seeking to kill and destroy. They want us to follow innocently into danger, often the very dangers about which we are clueless and naïve. And as much as we think we are safe and protected, danger is out there, lurking to enter our lives and take us where we should not go. Red didn't have enough life experience to cross that big highway like Brownie. He didn't know how to protect himself against deadly machines called cars. He went trustingly to follow his friend and biological father, and because he was unable to guard himself against the danger, he is gone. Completely gone. We can't let this be our story.

God, in His Alpha to Omega Word, gives us directions for how to protect ourselves in a world filled with deadly possibilities. He says that we must put on the armor of God and stand strong against the schemes of Satan: the fiery darts he sends our way. The armor is about putting on God's truth and righteousness, and it's about taking up the shield of faith and sword of the Spirit, which is the Word of God. But we can't do this if we sit in ignorance and don't *know* His Word. And we can't plead ignorance, like Red and Eliza, just because we didn't know better. There is no excuse for ignorance when His Word, designed to protect us against just such evil, is waiting to be read . . . waiting to be studied . . . waiting to be placed in our hearts. We must have His Word in our hearts every day, but especially on the days when Satan is seeking to destroy us and we need to know how to stop him. Ignorance is not bliss any more than my farm is a bubble of safety. It's an illusion and a dangerous one.

God is watching over His children --- you and me --- and like a good Father, He wants to protect us. But every time we refuse His protection and step outside His bubble, we find ourselves in a dangerous place. Now, I am NOT saying that if we walk closely with God, we will never have trouble. That's not what His Word says, but it does say that His word can protect us against sin, against evil attacks, and against following down a wrong path. His Word says that He will guide us if we just ask, and so often, we don't have His guidance because we're not asking. Like Red and Eliza, we're just blindly following what looks like fun, when the reality is that destruction is just beyond the bridge.

And unlike the fate of my sweet pets, destruction is not always immediate. Sometimes, like in certain areas of my life and maybe yours, it's a long, slippery slope toward a disastrous end. Maybe you eat to fill your emptiness, and it leads to serious weight and health issues. Maybe you drink to numb your pain, and it leads to more pain and addiction. Maybe you desperately seek people to fill your needs and find yourself lonely and empty when they let you down. Maybe you pour yourself completely into work, while losing your family and the precious time you have been given with them.

But it doesn't have to be this way.

In the Old Testament, when the children of Israel were grumbling and complaining about food, God gave them daily provision --- a daily portion of everything they needed. And I believe that's what we must remember: God will give us the perfect portion of exactly what we need if we allow Him to do so. In Lysa Terkeurst's *Made to Crave*, she says: "Each day God can be the perfect portion of everything we need --- every longing we have, every desperate desire our souls cry out for. God will be our portion." He can fill our need for companionship, strength, comfort, provision, patience . . . whatever we need, He can and will give if we but ask. We don't have to blindly follow someone across a highway of destruction when we have a loving Father waiting to give us His perfect gifts.

So today, I beg you to ask Him to provide. Ask Him for His safety, His provision, His comfort and joy. And put on the Truth of His Word: you are a child of the King of the world. No less! And because you belong to the King and have inherited your position as co-heir with Jesus Christ, you don't have to succumb to Satan's frantic efforts to compel you toward destruction. It doesn't have to be your destiny. Stand up against him this day and every day, asking God for His daily provision for all you need, and I know you will be safe in the arms of our Father.

Jake and the Bully

Years ago my youngest child, Jake, was in an elementary afterschool program. Jake is extremely easy-going, so when I arrived one day to see his frantic face, I knew something was wrong. Another boy had been bullying him, taking all of Jake's toys and stuffing them into his own pockets. He refused to give them back, and Jake felt helpless. The boy was bigger and way more aggressive. These items weren't anything expensive; they were just trinkets, but they mattered to Jake. My day in middle school had been particularly stressful, so my patience was definitely running on empty. Being the protective mom that I can be, I went straight to the other boy, insisted that he empty his pockets, and asked Jake if these items were his. They were. I didn't give the boy time to argue, in fact, I guess I sort of ambushed him, not in a physical way but by verbally assuming he was in the wrong and insisting that he give Jake his toys. He did, and we left, and on the way home, I asked Jake a question: "Where were your teachers when this was happening? Didn't they notice?" They didn't, not because they didn't care, but the playground was big and they were monitoring a very large area. The meanness slipped through the cracks, but then I arrived on the scene, handling both the situation and my son.

I felt like Jake's mighty warrior that afternoon, kind of like

God must feel when He protects us from the bullies in life. Jake was able to stand, watch, and "win" because I won, his protector. We can do the same because we have a Protector.

In Zephaniah 3: 17, we read these beautiful words:

> The Lord your God is among you,
>
> A warrior who saves.
>
> He will rejoice over you with gladness.
>
> He will be quiet in His love.
>
> He will delight in you with singing.

What an encouraging image of God! He is the warrior who saves, and even more, He delights in us with singing! Can you imagine God singing over you with delight? That is such a beautiful image that I can't help smiling when I think of it. But back to the bullies . . .

I don't know what's bullying you in your life today. Maybe it's a mean co-worker --- I've been there and done that one. Maybe it's a vicious boss who is unfair and rude to you. Been there, too. Maybe it's a spouse who treats you disrespectfully or a friend who constantly talks down to you. Maybe it's an internal bully . . . a bully called doubt, fear, insecurity . . . these bullies can beat you to pieces, but we have a God who says, "Enough!" He is our mighty warrior who saves us from the bullies. Does the bullying sometimes last a while? It does. Life is simply difficult, and when we are in unfair situations with others, we learn a lot about perseverance and trust in God. But here's what I know for sure: our mighty warrior WILL save us. He is a trustworthy, loving parent. And just like I demanded justice for Jake, He will do the same for us, but it will be in His way and His timing, both of which we don't always understand.

Yesterday I was listening to Joyce Meyer give her testimony (on television) about her childhood sexual abuse. I was actually in the audience when she taped that talk, and it stunned thousands of women into complete silence and quiet tears. But here's something she said that I'll never forget: she prayed for God to save her from her bully --- her father --- but she was not rescued from the situation. However, God gave her the strength to survive, and He used her experiences to make her into the mighty warrior for Him that she is today. She will tell you clearly that she would not change her life because God has used it for so much Kingdom good. It's hard to believe but it's true. Her childhood experiences with a bully made her able to have compassion and true empathy for people in pain, and God has used her to bring more people to Christ than I can even imagine. He has used her to feed thousands of hungry, hurting children and build homes for orphans. The list of ways she ministers to others goes on and on, and she uses her platform to share her painful story but only because her Protector gets all the credit and the glory. She is able to tell people from personal experience that God is indeed our mighty Warrior, the one who saves and heals! And there's nothing better than reading it in God's Word and seeing it in real life.

Today I encourage you to persevere against whatever bully you may be facing. If it is a situation from which you can remove yourself to safety, do it. But if, like Jake, you are helpless to win in this moment, call out to God, your Father and Protector, your mighty Warrior, the one who will save you, rejoice over you, and quiet your fearful heart with His incredible love. You are not alone, and though it may look like the bully is winning today, we know who wins the final victory, and praise God, we belong to the victor!

Jean B. Burden

A Frog in My Path

I detest frogs. I know it's irrational, but I'm scared of frogs . . . *hysterically* scared. I think it started when I was a little girl, and I had warts on both hands. The "science" of the day said that I must have played with frogs, who "peed" on me, giving me warts. (Don't stop reading; I promise that I will get to a point that isn't so gross!) Now, my brain knows the truth today: those frogs were not the problem, but I have hated them too long to change, and I simply don't see that I *have* to change. I'm sixty years old, and I don't have a need to love frogs, which brings me to a problem.

One day recently I went for a walk. I was wearing my headphones, singing praise songs and enjoying nature on our farm. And then it happened: I looked slightly down the path and saw a frog. He was planted right in the middle of the road, and I found myself in a dilemma. I could A: turn around and go home. B: walk over him. (Not happening!) C. find a way around him, trying not to panic with the thought that he could jump on me. None of these options were great, but they did set my brain to thinking about God: is there something God has anointed me --- or you --- to do, but we're stymied by a frog in our path? Hmmm . . . let's consider this frog-problem.

This morning as I went outside to pray, God impressed something on my heart: maybe the frog in my path is one I placed there. Is God asking me to do something, but I have put the frog of procrastination in my way? Or, have I allowed idolatry of any kind to seep into the road I'm walking, and God is waiting on me to remove the frog? Have I failed to forgive someone, or make amends with someone? Have I failed to pray with persistence, desperation, confidence and expectation, and my wimpy prayers have become a frog strangler to my dreams? It's easy to think we are waiting on God when sometimes, He is waiting on us to remove the very frog that's blocking His blessings. Other times, the frog comes from Satan. Same problem with a different ugly skin.

Satan throws frogs at us to thwart the plans of God, plans He has designed for us to bring Him glory. What are some Satan-frogs? Well, frogs called fear and anxiety. Scripture is clear that God did not give us these two frogs; instead He gave us a sound mind, and Jesus promised us peace. Satan can also throw a lack of confidence in our path . . . insecurity. . . a really ugly and debilitating frog. He tries to convince us that we are not good enough, worthy enough, or useful enough. Again, not true. Scripture tells us that we are not to lose our confidence . . . our holy confidence in a Sovereign God. We are worthy because He says so: worthy daughters and sons of the King of the world. Did your momma ever say to you, "Why? Because I said so!" and you believed it. Right? Well, we can't be shut down by frogs when our Father "says so!" And there are other frogs as well.

Frogs called doubt. Frogs called ego. Frogs called laziness. Frogs called . . . well, you know. Anything he can throw our way, in our path, to make us turn around and run for home.

I don't want to be a frog-runner; I want to be a God-victor. I can't afford a frog-mentality if I want to give myself completely to God, to be used for His glory, and neither can you. So what do we do?

First, we pray, asking God to reveal whatever it is that is blocking our path. Sometimes, you see, we don't even see it and we cannot deal with what we choose to ignore. Second, we pray for God to give us the strength and confidence to deal with the frog, whatever it is. If it is one of our own making, we ask God for help! God, help me remove this filthy frog from my life! If it's a frog from Satan, we ask the same, except we also make it clear to Satan that his frogs have no more power. Satan is a bully, and like all bullies, when his bluff is called, his power is gone. He may be loud and ugly and bumpy, but he *isn't* God.

Finally, we give ourselves completely to God, entrusting our lives and plans to the God who created us, loves us, and hungers to bless us. We give our hearts to Jesus, the Savior who chose to go straight to the Cross for you and me . . . no frogs in His path because He knew exactly what He had to do: the Father's will. You and I know it, too.

Today, seek God in prayer . . . first thing in the day and all day. Ask Him for His holy help, holy confidence, and holy strength. Ask Him for ways to remove the frog or step over him without fear. When I met the physical frog in my path, I did just that! ☺ I pray that you will join me in being frog-fearless!

Jean B. Burden

A Full House

Dan and I seem to attract strays. Or maybe people and animals just know we love and accept strays so they keep sending them to us. Either way we seem to be a growing family of people and animals who *need* a family, and that's just fine with us.

First, it was Brownie, who made himself at home (literally . . .), giving us two litters of puppies but not letting us touch him. He watched us from afar for over a year, sometimes sitting in a driving rain to keep his distance. For a while he left us, but then out of nowhere, he returned, still distant but in our line of vision. Today he is one of the family, allowing us to love on him unconditionally and sloppily, but I'll share his "coming home" story another day. Today it's about strays, which brings me to Athena.

Athena is one of three kittens that my son, Jake, fed at our old house while he was living there. When Jake moved to our new home a few months ago, he brought the kittens with him. Athena came pretty easily but sadly, the others never adjusted. With each passing day, Athena has become more and more comfortable with our home situation, and today you can find her in the garage with the four dogs, resting in peace and confidence that this is her home, too. But I'm not done yet because there's Rocky.

Rocky was dropped here (with permission!) by a dear friend, Becky. He showed up at her house uninvited, and she was not in a place to keep another cat. After she and her husband brought him here, he took off and we didn't see him for about six days. But one day, out of the blue, he showed up again at our "little house," and Jake, my cat whisperer, managed to feed him. Like Brownie, he is nervous about people, but he has found a forever home here on Boggy Road. We can get within about

six inches of him, feed him, and talk to him, but no touching so far. One day, he'll come around, and in the meantime, he knows he has found his permanent family. And this brings me to the people in our lives.

Sometimes God brings friends or new family members into our lives because they need us. They need what we have to offer, and God knows what we have to give. Sometimes it's acceptance, and other times it's simply a listening ear. Sometimes it's an act of kindness, a smile, or resources that we can offer. Whatever it is, I know this: God doesn't bring people to us accidentally. He knows exactly the partnerships that work for His people, and He places people before us as an opportunity to love others the way He loves us. He sets God-ordained appointments for us, and our task is to respond to whatever He places before us. I don't think we have to hunt for people; God's amazing sovereignty and providence place people exactly where they need to be to receive the love and grace they so desperately crave.

So what is our task? Pay attention. Pray, asking God to make you alert and aware of what's happening around you, a need He is asking you to meet. Treat others in a way that brings glory to God, our Father. Keep an open heart and make a decision to be obedient, because when you do, you might be helping others but I promise, you will be blessed beyond measure!

A Journey of Faith

Dan and I visited a church in West Yarmouth, MA, (on Cape Cod) in the Summer of 2017, and we heard a sermon that captured my thoughts. I love the *Wizard of Oz* story, which was the catalyst for her sermon, so here are some things to ponder today as you worship and reflect on God.

Faith-walking can be frightening, and every step brings the possibility of tripping and falling. We meet people on our path who can be our fellow pilgrims on this journey. Think about it like this.

In *The Wizard of Oz*, Dorothy is on a journey of seeking, starting with only one friend, her dog, Toto. She doesn't know where she is going, and even when she has a destination in mind, she only has a "road" to take her there but not much direction otherwise. She has to accept pieces and parts of information along the way.

Key Truth: God gives us a road to walk and does not always show us the big picture. We have to trust His "road" in pieces, knowing that He is with us.

She meets the Scarecrow . . . Dorothy had to help him, just as he helped her get through danger on the road. She had to reassure him, "re-stuffing" him along the way, but they kept going together.

Key Truth: We need others who can "re-stuff" us when life empties us, steals from us, and leaves us damaged by the roadside.

She meets the Tin Man . . . he was stuck. Without a friend to "oil" him, he couldn't make progress. Dorothy oils his joints, he breaks loose, and they continue on the journey side by side. All he wanted was a heart and love, and he found it with Dorothy.

Key Truth: We all need help lubricating our thinking so we aren't "stuck" in a rut of life, and friends help to do that.

She meets the cowardly lion . . . he wants courage because it takes courage to risk new things and because he wants to be what he is expected to be. Dorothy and friends help him find his courage within and he finds that he is no longer afraid to be in relationship with others.

Key Truth: It takes courage to open our hearts to others, but when we do, we allow them to give us new strength we don't think we have.

They slept in the field of poppies . . . we all need a "holy rest" . . . to stop, look, and rest for the journey. "He makes me lie down beside green pastures, He leads me beside still waters, He restores my soul."

Key Truth: We must rest in the "field" of God's safety and grace.

The big Key Truth: we so often have within us the very things we are seeking . . . a heart, a brain, courage, and a place of safety to land . . . a place called home. God has already placed gifts within us, and we must recognize them, allowing others to help us cultivate our God-given gifts as we journey through life. And most importantly? We must know that our heavenly home is always waiting. Like Dorothy, we *MUST* be homesick for home . . . our *final* home.

We, as people of God, must find others who will journey with us on the path of life. We are not meant to do this pilgrimage alone; we need encouragers, accountability partners, and those who love us, even when we fall, pushing us to keep going and growing.

It ALL matters on the journey of faith.

----Thanks to Rev. Teresa Sterling, fill-in pastor for the day at The Congregational Church of West Yarmouth, MA. I added my thoughts but she created the bones of this message. Be blessed today and let others share your journey.

Jean B. Burden

A New Month . . . and It's War!

I am writing this on November 1. Another month has passed . . . another cycle of the moon . . . another hurricane is in the books, leaving tremendous devastation in its wake . . . another angel has made her way to heaven . . .lives altered.

Time and events march forward like an army of soldiers headed to war.

And this *IS* war.

Don't miss this one: **we are at war.** I'm not talking about ISIS or Al-Qaeda. I'm not talking about nuclear weapons or political wrangling. I'm talking about all-out war for our lives.

In *Waking the Dead*, John Eldredge tells us that one of the biggest mistakes of the Christian is not to believe that we are in a war for our lives, allowing ourselves to become complacent and soft while Satan does his worst. *Damage* and *devastation* are his middle names. *Devour* is his mantra. And even worse, he doesn't work alone. He has demonic forces assisting him in his sole purpose: to destroy anything and everything that would cause us to worship our one true God.

Recently, my women's Bible study group has been studying the story of Gideon, a warrior chosen by God to fight the

Midianites, and homework one night asked us to look at our circles of influence. I did the homework . . .checked off my "to-do" list . . . but it wasn't until this morning that the Holy Spirit brought that homework into my heart in a very real way. And in listening to the Holy Spirit, I was reminded of some urgent truths.

1) We can study God's Word all we want, but it's in taking that study to God and asking the Holy Spirit to speak to us that we begin to *own* what we've studied. In other words, study without prayer is just okay, but it's not powerful until we bathe it in petitions to God.

2) The people in my circles of influence --- both near and far --- are suffering damage from Satan's schemes, often completely unaware that he is winning. It becomes so clear when we lift them in prayer. It is my job --- our job --- to be prayer warriors, intercessors, for those around us, and it is a privilege God has given to every believer.

3) We have God-given weapons to be wielded against Satan, but when we don't use them, we are foolishly wasting the power left to us when Jesus ascended into heaven.

4) Praying for ourselves, our families, our friends, and the world requires long obedience in one direction. We can't pray once and then be disappointed when God doesn't answer. In the opposite vein, we can't pray, see God's answer, and then fail to thank Him. Prayer and thanksgiving require long obedience in

the direction of God, and they are mighty powerful weapons against the enemy. Scripture says that praise brings down walls!

At the time of this writing, my church was studying the Kyle Idleman book, *not a fan*. One day's homework asked us to repeat this phrase throughout the day: "Lord, interfere in my life." A powerful statement, if we really mean it. "Lord, interfere in my life . . ." by softening my heart toward my enemies, by giving me a fighting spirit against Satan's schemes, by giving me a task to complete that I don't necessarily see myself doing, by giving me a hunger to tell others about You, by convicting me of my apathy and complacency about my faith, by shining Your light in the dark places of my heart . . . "Lord, interfere with my life and the lives of those in my sphere of influence." We're supposed to repeat this one-line prayer throughout the day, and in repeating it, keep ourselves in constant contact with our Savior. And here's what I know: when Jesus interferes in my daily walk, things *will* begin to happen, both in me and in those for whom I am praying. "Lord, interfere in my life, and make me a warrior-daughter of the King!"

And that's what we are . . . we are not apathetic wimps; we are **Warriors**, able to fight with the armor of God for ourselves, our families, our friends, our neighbors, our communities, our states, our world, our politicians . . . *yes*, our politicians. And when we fight back, we can stand in the assurance that God hears our prayers and will answer.

I beg you today: **fight** for your family and friends. **Fight** for our nation. **Fight** for yourself as you step into the God-ordained destiny of making a difference for the Kingdom. **Be strong** in the Lord . . . which reminds me of a favorite hymn:

Be strong in the Lord, and be of good courage; your mighty Defender is always the same.

Mount up with wings, as the eagle ascending; victory is sure when you call on His name.

Be strong, be strong, be strong in the Lord,

And be of good courage, for He is Your guide.

Be strong, be strong, be strong in the Lord, and rejoice for the victory is yours!

So put on the armor the Lord has provided, and place your defense in His unfailing care.

Trust Him for He will be with you in battle, lighting your path to avoid every snare.

Be strong, be strong, be strong in the Lord,

And be of good courage, for He is Your guide.

Be strong, be strong, be strong in the Lord, and rejoice for the victory is yours!

[Linda Lee Johnson, 1979: Hope Publishing Company]

Jean B. Burden

Awed by Creation

As I am writing this piece, I've been at the beach for a week, and God always speaks into my heart when I spend time at the ocean. Of course, there are the obvious things . . . the ocean is an incredible part of God's creation and it is beautiful, but there's more. Indulge me and please read on . . .

Lesson #1: The ocean is a visible example of God's consistency. As Dan and I walked the beach yesterday morning, I watched the waves as they rolled in and washed out, and their constancy never fails. I understand that there is science behind the reason the tides occur and waves come to the shore, but God created the science, and the science only serves to magnify Him! Surely He must have wanted us to have an in-your-face experience with something that never fails, something that never leaves us, something that calls out to us from the deep . . . something just like Him. God never fails; He never leaves us; He calls out to us from the deep, beckoning us to step into the waters of a faith-filled life with Him. And does He quit beckoning simply because we are afraid to put our feet in His water? No, He keeps calling our names no matter how long it takes us to respond. Four of my granddaughters visited me at the beach this week, and one of them had serious reservations about the waves. She wouldn't go with the others when they ventured into the deep, but by Friday, she gave in to the call of the waters and the joy they give. God is still calling you, even if you have been afraid to answer, and when you step into the water with Him, you will find joy!

Lesson #2: The ocean is a visible reminder of God's power. Yesterday as I stood with my feet in the water, looking for beautiful treasures, the water almost knocked me over quite a few times, and more than once I was reminded that God's power is evident there. And of course, we know that

when we go out into the deep water, the pull is even more powerful, just as it is with God when we accept His call to step into the depths of His love. Even in the shallow water, my granddaughters were being pulled by the current, away from our chairs on the beach. . . . they were being pulled and they didn't even realize it. God's powerful love is like that. He is pulling and calling and desiring a relationship with you, and maybe you don't even realize it. Ask Him to help you recognize His power and love at work in your life!

Lesson #3: There are tiny treasures to be found when we pay attention. On our first trip to the sand, amidst the billions of shells, I found three sharks' teeth in a matter of minutes. But I only found them because I was looking, and God's treasures are that way, too. He is waiting and hungering to bless us with treasures, both great and small, but we need to be on the lookout. Sometimes, in the words of Squire Rushnell, author of *When God Winks*, it is a small "wink" and we can miss it if we are not paying attention because those little things can get lost in the billion other things that try to capture our minds and hearts. So I encourage you to do two things: first, slow down and notice. Just notice the things God is doing for you and placing in your line of vision. Second, start a blessings journal so you don't lose sight of the small treasures God allows in your day.

Lesson #4, and the last: The ocean is a visible reminder of the enormity of God and His creation, and the sheer size of it all overwhelms me. We read in Genesis that He created all of this, and it was and is good . . . the vastness of it all incomprehensible. Though I know the ocean has an end, I cannot see it when I am standing on the beach; it appears to be infinite, reminding me of God's infinite love. And when I stand in the water's edge with my feet among the billions of tiny pieces of shells, again I am awed by a number I cannot even fathom. If I can see thousands right at my feet, how many more are there beyond my vision, in the deep recesses of the ocean? And this tells me so much about God. He is everything and more. He is the Alpha and the Omega, the beginning and the end, and He has always been with us. His power and might are grander than I can understand, and He is omnipresent . . . we cannot go anywhere that God is not present because He is everywhere. The enormity of His reach and His power stun me because in contrast, I also remember that He loves me . . . little me in Conway, SC. Little you, wherever you are. This enormous God of an enormous creation also loves us and knows us individually. It's almost too much to comprehend, but in faith and experience, I stand on this truth. He is an omnipotent, omnipresent, sovereign God of the entire universe who is also capable of knowing our hearts one-on-one. Amazing.

And this brings me to the question: Do you know Him? Have you accepted His call to be in relationship with Him? To meet Him in the deep places of worship and adoration? To accept His sacrificial gift of His only Son to be your Savior? If you have not, He is still calling. He is calling from the vastness of creation, and He wants to *know* you. He already loves you; He needs you to accept His gift of grace and love, and love Him back. Maybe your words today need to be, "I love you, too, God," because when you look at creation, you have to know that He has been sending His love letter to us since the beginning of time.

And here endeth the reflections of a woman who is grateful to be standing in the deep with God, the Father, and praying to go deeper still as He continues to call me. I pray that, like me, you will answer Him today.

Jean B. Burden

Bloom When It's Time

For years I have heard the saying, "Bloom where you are planted," and I agree with the statement. However, I've been thinking a lot lately about seasons of life, and right now, I hear a new saying in my heart: Bloom when it's time.

As I walked my daylily garden this morning, I took notice of something that is always there but caught my eye and heart today: some flowers are in full bloom, others are finished for the season, and some have not even begun to show buds. In the daylily world, these are labeled by the portion of the season in which they bloom: early, early-mid, middle, mid-late, and late. It's so nice to have flowers blooming throughout the entire season, and I found myself pondering this concept of blooming when it's time. It works for flowers, and it works for us, too.

When I was a middle school teacher, I bloomed and flourished in the classroom because it was my clear calling from God. When I started singing and speaking to women's groups, I unexpectedly found myself blooming joyfully in those venues as well. A few years ago, after retiring from public education, I received invitations to teach at the college level, and I found myself blooming in new and different locations. Once again, I knew I was flourishing because God opened those doors and placed me there. Now I find myself in a waiting season . . . being weeded, watered and fertilized because I believe God is preparing me to bloom somewhere new. He has shown Himself in some very dark days recently, and He has forced me to practice lots of patience. Not always fun but necessary. After all, I can't bloom before my time. He has humbled me in a couple of situations and reminded me over and over to trust His plan for my blooming season. And just like my inability to make daylilies bloom before their natural time, I cannot force God's plan to "bloom" in my life before He has everything ready. Oh, I can try and push . . . and ruin things.

And so I wait.

But in the waiting, here's what I do, and what you need to do if you are waiting on a new blooming season as well. First, give God your hopes and dreams . . . completely. Entrust them to Him because He always knows what's best, and often, He returns those dreams to us in a better form than we could possibly envision. Remember Ephesians 3: 20-21: Now to Him who is able to do more than I can ask or imagine . . .? Well, that's our God; He can and He will.

Second, pray in the waiting. Spend part of every day in prayer, making sure to praise Him in the hallway of life until He opens a new door. In the Old Testament (2 Chronicles 20:21), we read this: "Then he [Jehoshaphat] consulted with the people and appointed some to sing for the LORD and some to praise the splendor of His holiness. When they went out in front of the armed forces, they kept singing: Give thanks to the LORD, for His faithful love endures forever." The choir led the way, singing praises as they went into battle. Amazing and effective. We need to praise God, our Father, every day, but especially when we are headed into something difficult or challenging . . . something like waiting on a new direction from God. Praise Him in the splendor of His holiness, and keep singing about His faithful love. It is, indeed, faithful.

And third, while you are waiting, don't be passive. Be active for God. You might be waiting on specific instructions from God about a plan for your life, but in the meantime, you and I know what to do in *every* season. **Love** people everywhere you go, planting seeds of God's love in a hurting world. **Stay in church**. We are told clearly to "not stop meeting together" because it is with God's people that we find strength for the journey and accountability. **Pay attention** to what God is already doing around you and offer support if you feel led. **Listen** to someone who needs a listening ear and a kind face. **Pray** with people who may not know the power of prayer but desperately need an intercessor. **Study** His Word to know Him more and to be ready for the work He is calling you to do. The list is endless . . . we *know* what we are supposed to do, even when God may be taking us in a new direction. And I believe this: when we are faithful to love and study and pray and be a light in this dark world, God is with us at every step, and as we mature in the waiting, God is preparing us to bloom with colors and beauty we cannot even fathom.

So, yes, bloom where you are planted, but also know that God will put you in new places to bloom according to His timetable, and it will be beautiful!

Choosing a Door

If you are my age, I'm sure you remember a ridiculous, but fun television show called "Let's Make a Deal." Audience members dressed in crazy costumes, hoping to get a chance to make a deal with the host, Monty Hall. One particular "deal" involved three doors; the contestant was told to choose one of the doors. Behind two of the three doors were undesirable prizes, if you can even call them prizes... things like goats or llamas, prizes made even more worthless because they could not be taken home. But there was always one door with a *real* prize behind it --- a trip, a car, a washer and dryer --- something tangible that caused contestants to scream and shout and make fools of themselves for just a minute because the prize they found was worth having.

In life there are doors for us as well, and only one has the best "yes" behind it . . . something worth rejoicing over . . . the thing God has designed just for you or me.

Too often in life we fill our days with myriad activities and appointments that, in the long run, don't amount to much. Oh, they might give us some fun, a little glory, and even momentary pleasure, and there is absolutely nothing wrong with doing things we enjoy as long as they don't go against God's word. Some tasks, of course, *must* be done . . . laundry, dishes, and my absolute most hated one: dusting. But then we often fail to leave margin in our days just to seek God and breathe in His presence. Pages of books have margins for a purpose: they keep the pages from being too crowded for the eye and brain to absorb. Margins in life do that for us as well. They keep some white space in our days, spaces intentionally left empty so we can find peace, seek God, and listen to His call. Why? Because we need to hear His voice if we are to choose the right door --- the one designed by our Creator --- the one with the tasks and blessings behind it that are meant specifically and individually for each one of us. Oh, yes, God will let us choose and open the wrong doors, and we will find some junk there --- possibly junk with bad consequences. Sometimes we will even find some good things, but the problem is this: if we don't listen to our Father's voice in choosing, we will get a prize but even if it is good, it won't be great. It can't be perfect and won't be the very thing He has custom designed with our gifts in mind. I can almost hear the buzzer from Let's Make a Deal, signifying that a person has chosen a dud door.

I don't want a dud door . . . for me or for you. I also don't want *almost* perfect; I want the perfect will of God. I want to choose the perfect door for me, knowing that when I do, God will use its contents for His glory. I desperately want the same thing for you.

And there's another door image in scripture that's even more vital than this.

In the book of John, we hear numerous statements about Jesus, and it never says that He is "a" door. It clearly states that He is "the" door. The *only* door to God. The *only* door to salvation. In John 10:7, Jesus says, "Let me assure you: I am the door." Another translation says, "I am the gate." Same idea. He is the only way to God. Later in John 14:6, we read this: "I am the Way, the Truth and the Life. No one comes to the Father except through Me." Sounds like the right door, huh? The *only* door if we want to have eternal life in heaven with God the Father and Jesus the Son.

I chose to walk through the door to Jesus many years ago; I have faltered and failed Him, but I have never regretted walking through the gate toward the Shepherd. And for years now, I have been seeking His choices of doors for me . . . choices that have changed in various seasons of my life, but one thing has never wavered: choosing Jesus and choosing God's will for my life have blessed me in ways I cannot begin to fully comprehend. Walking in His paths for us gives God the glory and allows us to be used in the kingdom.

If you have not answered the call from Christ to walk through the door to salvation and you need to talk to someone about this decision, do it. Don't wait. Just do it. And if you are pondering a choice, a next step, or a decision, seek God's voice before you walk through a door that might be dangerous or might be just average. Don't settle for anything less than the doors God is trying to open for you. It will be the best deal you will ever find!

Comfort Foods and Such

I woke up this morning in a funk. I think I know the reason, but understanding it or not, I still found myself in a weird, discouraging funk. So, I did what I often do when I'm feeling a little off . . . I turned to a comfort food: Brown Sugar Cinnamon Pop Tarts. I know . . . ridiculous calories and not at all good for me, but I ate it anyway because it is a comfort food when life is beating at the door. Mashed potatoes are another (or actually *any* potato cooked *any* way!). I feel sure that the sense of comfort comes from the fact that my mother used to give me both on a regular basis, and her homemade mashed potatoes were amazing; I can almost taste them right now. And when I ate those foods along with others like Campbell's Tomato Soup and hot grits with butter, they became connected in my heart and mind with the protective feel of my relationship with my mom and the peace I always felt in her home. Well, she is gone, my dad is gone, and the home is gone, so in my moments of weakness, I turn to those foods that remind me of the comfort I so desperately miss. And then, I remember that there is comfort to be found in God.

I am reading a wonderful book called *The Daniel Key* by Anne Graham Lotz. In this book she shares twenty concepts we can learn from the book of Daniel . . . concepts we need to apply daily in our lives. In one chapter, she discusses worship, and she gave me an idea that was slightly new to me: when we are struggling with something specific, it is good to worship God for the very thing He is that we need at that moment in time. For example, if I need comfort, then I need to worship Him as the great Comforter, the one who holds my tears in His bottle and records my heartbreak in His record. Worship is all about honoring God for who He is --- His attributes, His sovereignty, His omnipotence and omnipresence . . . everything that defines *who He is*. In opening my prayer with this kind of worship, I am reminded of what He can and will do for me when I seek Him with all my heart. Needing comfort? Worship Him as the great Comforter. And then, turn to His word. In Psalm 119:76, we find this: *May Your unfailing love be my comfort, according to Your promise to Your servant.* And then in the 23rd Psalm, we find the words so many of us have memorized: *Even though I walk through the darkest valley, I will fear no evil, for you are with me; Your rod and Your staff, they comfort me.* In the Ephesians passage on the armor of God, we are told to wield the Sword of the Spirit, which is the Word of God. I often pray God's very words back to Him . . . "God, you promised to be my comfort through the dark valleys, and I need You now."

People find comfort everywhere, and many of the places are unhealthy and come with collateral damage. Reorient your face toward God today, worshiping Him as the God of all comfort who sustains us through . . . well, every funk. ☺

Damaged and Beautiful

If you follow my writings, you probably know a little about Brownie, our "visiting" dog. Well, Brownie is no longer a visitor but an integral part of our family and our hearts. You've heard the line, "He came, he saw, he conquered"? Well, that's just what he did, only he stayed when the tasks were complete. Brownie found our Boggy Road home because our two female labs were in heat. He hung around long enough to leave Bella and Eliza expecting puppies, but then he did something I find quite unusual for a visiting dog: he hung around to watch the girls throughout the pregnancy and delivery. Of course, I began feeding him, but I could never get close enough to touch him. During the winter of 2017, he finally risked a night in our garage to escape the cold, and my husband found him the next morning, trapped in the corner with no way out. Dan rubbed him while he trembled in fear. The next day, the same event happened, only this time it was with me. Again, he trembled in fear and dread, but he did allow me to rub his head. Over time, Brownie began to trust us, but *only* us. Friends and family could not get near him . . . only his new owners. By spring he began to let the grandchildren rub his back, and just recently, he even allowed one of my Bible study friends to caress him gently. So the question becomes this: why did it take so long to get

Brownie to allow us into his close circle? Why was trust so hard to achieve with him? Who damaged him so badly that he trembled in fear when dealing with humans?

And isn't this the same question with numbers of people we see in the world every day? Aren't people damaged by life and by people in one way or another? And what is our necessary response? Well, let's look to the scriptures where we find a clear model of what to do.

Over and over Jesus modeled His love and compassion for damaged, broken people. Remember Zacchaeus, the hated tax-collector? Jesus went home with him. Remember the woman at the well? She went to the well in the heat of the day just to avoid human contact. But Jesus? He spoke to her in peace and love, sharing His acceptance and forgiveness. Remember doubting Thomas? (a misnomer, in my humble opinion). Jesus didn't rebuke him; he showed him his nail-scarred hands and pierced side, and Thomas believed. Jesus didn't run him away because he dared to doubt. Remember the many others? The prostitute, the haters, the sinners, the ones damaged by life's events and their own sin? What was Jesus' response? Was it condemnation and rejection, or was it loving acceptance? I dare to think that you know the answer to that rhetorical question. So what is it we must do in a broken and hurting world?

Let's go back to Brownie. Once Dan and I touched him, we continued to lovingly and gently touch him every day until he was no longer trembling in fear but with shaking with delight. We fed him, loved him, and talked to him with tender voices. I told him every single day that he was safe and loved and had come to the right forever home. I held his head in my hands and spoke love through words and actions until he believed. Then, as he became less afraid over time, others have been able to do the same for him. Slowly? Yes. But progress? Oh, yes. Today he waits in our garage every morning, anxious to see our faces; he rests under a shade tree while we work in the yard; he reaps the benefits of being in a loving family. And I believe this same intentional plan works for people, too.

Last week in one of my college classes, my students asked me about how to handle very difficult students, and this led to a conversation about why young children can behave in such mean and disrespectful ways in school. And my response was what it always is: that child did not come into the world desiring to be mean and ugly. Something happened and may still be happening throughout his/her young life to create the product we see: the angry, bullying, disengaged, or frightened child. During a study of the story of Esther, Beth Moore said something I will never forget: "Meanness has a history." Just as Brownie has a history we will never know, people have the same kind of background. Does this mean that we allow them to bully and abuse us? No. But what it does mean is that as Christians, we have a responsibility to love them differently, just as Jesus loves us radically. We must be patient and gentle, not creating more hurt and damage in their lives. We must reach out to them without judgment so they stop trembling inside and allow us to reach into their worlds. We must look at them through "Jesus glasses," seeing beyond the outward ugliness, straight through to their empty and needy hearts. And what they need may not be *us*; we are simply the means to an end . . . a relationship with a compassionate, loving, forgiving Savior who is the ultimate Healer of all things broken. In the words of a talk I have heard many times on Emmaus weekends, we must be the hands and feet of Christ in a broken world because, after all, we are the *only* hands and feet He has. In fact, in Matthew we read these words straight from Jesus:

"Then the King will say to those on his right, 'Come, you who are blessed by my Father; take your inheritance, the kingdom prepared for you since the creation of the world. [35] For I was hungry and you gave me something to eat, I was thirsty and you gave me something to drink, I was a stranger and you invited me in, [36] I needed clothes and you clothed me, I was sick and you looked after me, I was in prison and you came to visit me.'

[37] "Then the righteous will answer him, 'Lord, when did we see you hungry and feed you, or thirsty and give you something to drink? [38] When did we see you a stranger and invite you in, or needing clothes and clothe you? [39] When did we see you sick or in prison and go to visit you?'

[40] "The King will reply, 'Truly I tell you, whatever you did for one of the least of these brothers and sisters of mine, you did for me." (Matthew 25:34-40 NIV)

And may I add a Jean-translation: Whatever you did for the broken and damaged of the world to bring them to Me (Christ), you did it for Me.

Requires no other explanation. Be His hands and feet in a world where damaged can become beautiful when we do as Christ commanded. Find the "Brownies" in your life, and gently draw them with the transforming love of Christ. It may take patience and time, but isn't it worth it? I know it is.

Jean B. Burden

Going Back Is Hard!

Last week I returned to yoga class after taking a one-year sabbatical. It was actually a year of having way too much work to do and feeling like I was drowning most of the time. I know yoga is good for me both physically and spiritually, and I know it helps my arthritis, but I still let it slip away, losing an urgent place in my schedule. Teaching at the colleges and traveling for my other job kept me on the road and quite honestly, exhausted. Completely exhausted. My writing suffered, my body suffered, and my spirit felt depleted. But I have retired from most of the work, and I am finding my way again, starting with writing, studying, and yes, yoga. But the yoga sure is hard.

On my third day back I attended what was supposed to be the easiest class of the week, but halfway through, I knew I was in trouble. Part of it was physical, but the other part was mental: I knew I had lost physical strength and stamina, and I couldn't seem to keep my mind "on the mat." By the end of class, I sunk into the mat and slipped quietly into tears. Not a pretty sight or a good feeling.

But the next day . . . (there is always another day, Scarlet!) . . . I went back. It was easier, and I think my mind was more prepared simply because I *did* go back. Having the grit to return gave me a renewed hope and a restored attitude. The muscles stretched more easily and the poses, though challenging, were attainable. The solution to never feeling this way again? Consistency.

When we walk away from consistently doing the very practices that are best for us, especially spending time with God and studying His word, it can be really hard to return; the difficulty can be similar to my return to yoga: challenging and a little tearful.

So why do we get lazy about spending time with God and His Word? We *know* it's good for us. We *know* it helps us to know Him. We *know* it stretches our minds and hearts, making us more like Him. We *know* that prayer makes a difference. And yet, we *still* walk away sometimes, letting life get in the way and overwhelm us until we eliminate the very thing that is the most important and makes the most difference in our days. So again, I ask, *why* do we do this? Well, I believe it's because we are human . . . fallible, weak humans. I also believe that in our weakness, Satan slips into our minds, convincing us that we don't have time for that morning devotional or that quiet time with God. He distracts us, not necessarily with evil things, but with to-do lists, and daily problems, and television, and . . . well, anything he can use to take us away from giving God first place in our day. We know better than to let him win; we just don't always do better; in the business world, it's called the knowing-doing gap. But there's good news.

God doesn't stop showing up for us, just because we stop

showing up for Him. Just like when I returned to yoga and the instructor was there, just like always, so is God. He is there to challenge us, strengthen us, teach us, and yes, let us cry "on the mat" when it's all we can do. And just like my yoga instructors are allowing me to take baby steps as I make my way back, God does that as well. He isn't there to condemn but to love us --- the prodigals --- and throw a party because we were lost for a moment and now are found. Isn't He just the best? My yoga instructor hugged me when I returned, and my peers welcomed me back with the sweetest, most genuine greetings, and God does the same. He is so glad to hear our voices reaching out to Him and see us putting our spiritual muscles back to work. No nasty comments because we got lost for a bit . . . just a welcoming Father who has missed us and is glad we're home.

In one of my previous books, I shared a piece from a favorite children's story, *Cat, You Better Come Home*. The rhyming chorus says this:

"O CAT, YOU BETTER COME HOME. You're a top cat now and you're riding high but they'll dump you in the river when the well runs dry, so CAT, YOU BETTER COME HOME."

Life will definitely dump us in the river, leaving us drowning and desperate to go home, and the wonderful news? Just like the cat's owner, God is waiting for you to come home. Don't hesitate because you've wandered . . . your decisions don't change God's unending, boundless love for you.

So, friend, head home. Head home. Head home. Remember Dorothy? There's no place like it. ☺

Jean B. Burden

Good Friday Thankfulness

I happen to be writing this on Good Friday, and I cannot help but think about how blessed I am. Not to say that we haven't had our difficulties because we have, but God has blessed us beyond measure, and today I am more grateful than ever. Jesus chose to suffer for us and redeem what we could not, and now, He is seated at the right hand of God, the Father, interceding for us as we pray and seek God's will for our lives. The journey has its challenges, but the journey with God is always good.

I am so thankful for so many things that I cannot name them, but today I am especially thankful for Christ, the church in which I serve, my dear friends, the fact that my daughter and her beautiful family are on the way home, my daughters and sons and their families who will welcome the Texans back to SC, spring and growing things, singing, breaking ground on a new home where Dan and I will continue to love each other, grow together, and enjoy our family and our faith.

Holy Week always reminds me that we must be over-the-top thankful for all that God has allowed in our lives, even the challenges because they have helped us to grow in His image. I hunger to honor Him with my time, my energy, my life, and my actions. He has done more than we could ever repay, but we can surely love Him completely and supremely and then act on that love.

I encourage you on Good Friday and every day to remember the sacrifice made for you and be thankful that Jesus was willing to walk the road we could not walk, pay the price we could not pay, and face the Cross we could not bear. He did it for us, and He loves us in ways we cannot even comprehend until we see Him face to face. Let your love for Him flow from you like a living stream to the others in your life for whom you are grateful. See your blessings and stop to thank Him today and every day.

Written on Good Friday, 2016

A Grandmother's Dreams

In the past two weeks I have suffered with some disturbing dreams about one of my granddaughters. In the first dream I think we were in Disney; she walked into an open door to take a look (maybe into a theater?), and I didn't stop her; I let her walk away. I panicked when I realized that she wasn't by my side, and though I looked everywhere, even in our hotel room, she couldn't be found. I began imagining the worst and wondering how I would ever tell her parents that I was careless and lost one of their most precious possessions. Finally, I woke up in a sweat and quickly reminded myself, "She's fine. It's a dream. It isn't real." Cool . . . moving on. But then came another dream about her.

In the second dream, I was walking down an unfamiliar street with her sister, and I saw her on a porch. I didn't recognize this porch, but I knew immediately that she was somehow with another family. I reached out across the white picket rails but couldn't reach her. She wasn't upset; *I* was. I simply wanted her to come back to us. Again, I awoke, but this time, I couldn't dismiss the dream, and so, I asked God, "What are you trying to tell me? Should I be concerned for her safety, or is this about something even greater?"

Definitely about something greater, but yes, about safety as well.

As I pondered and prayed about the possibilities of what God might be saying, two things were spoken into my spirit. I pray that I am hearing this correctly so I can share it with you.

First, people wander away from God all the time . . . even those who claim to love Him. The prodigal wandered away from his family and father, and he found himself in the most dire, desperate pigsty of situations. And don't we do that? Lily was drawn into the theater, away from her Grandma, by something alluring and beautiful, and we are compelled toward surface-beauty as well. But what happens is that in walking aimlessly toward something that looks pretty on the outside, we can walk away from God and right into being lost. Lost from family, lost from friends, and most importantly, lost from God. Let me be clear: He *always* knows where *we* are, but He gives us the choice to be foolish and walk away from Him and His protection. The prodigal's father is a perfect picture of God; he allowed his son to take his inheritance, walk away, and squander it foolishly, but when his son wanted to return home, his father welcomed him with open arms and a party. I'm sure that if I had found Lily at the end of my dream, I would have thrown a celebration as well, and God does that every single time one of us . . . the wanderers . . . returns to His fold. He celebrates with a holy shout, but there's something for us to do as well.

As God's children who love Him, we are responsible for being proactive and preventative in our lives, doing everything in our power not to allow ourselves and those in our care or sphere of influence to walk away into danger. It is our job to love, to pray fervently, and to know and teach them a foundation based on God's love and grace. Will we or others still wander? Yes, it will happen, but we must be diligent guards, staying closely connected to God and those we love, asking Him always to keep them close and doing our part to ground them in His truth.

And then there's the lesson of the second dream: there will come a time when we will see our loved ones "on the porch," cut off from us and headed toward eternal damnation with another family NOT of God. There will come a time when it will be too late to "train them up in the way they should go." When Jesus returns, the Bible is clear: those who have rejected Christ as the only way to God the Father will live in eternal separation from God . . . the worst hell imaginable. So what is our job that God has impressed upon me through this dream?

We must go, tell, and live in such a way that our family, friends, co-workers, and strangers with whom we come in contact see and hear the grace of a living, breathing God who is waiting expectantly for them to kneel at His feet, bask in His love, and live safely in His arms. Our job is to share the message of the love of a Savior who would choose a Cross on our behalf . . . take punishment He didn't deserve . . . die for our guilty souls. Oh, what love! And it is our task to share that love through words and actions so no one gets "lost on the porch" of life without God.

In recent days I have been praying quite a bit about people I love who have never walked with God or have wandered away from Him. These dreams have placed a renewed fervency in my heart and spirit to do the very thing Jesus told us to do: Go ye therefore and teach all nations, baptizing them in the name of the Father, the Son, and the Holy Spirit, teaching them to observe all things . . . And all nations begins at home with our spouses, our children, our grandchildren, our friends, our co-workers, our enemies. . . **everyone.** We simply cannot be careless, allowing people to wander away without our paying attention, and we cannot sit idly by, failing to pray tenaciously that they will give themselves over to God, allowing Him to be the Lord of their lives. It's easy to put this off, but tomorrow could be too late; we are not promised days --- we are promised *grace . . . amazing grace.* Don't let another moment go by without lifting yourself and others to the throne of God, creating a prayer storm of worship, praise and petitions until every single wanderer is drawn onto the only porch that saves: the porch of heaven.

He's Everywhere!

Recently I had four of my seven grandchildren for the day; they range in age from two to seven years old, all girls. As we prepared to eat lunch, saying a prayer for the food, a conversation erupted about where God is. I told them that God is everywhere, and I even had them learn a new vocabulary word: *omnipresence.* Then one of them asked me, "So, can He sit at this table with us?"

"Of course," I answered. "He goes with us all the time, no matter where we go or what we do. He is there watching over us and loving us."

After that the conversation got a little silly about God protecting lamps and chairs . . . ahhh, life with giggling little children. ☺

But this morning, this concept of omnipresence came up twice more. I knew right then that the Holy Spirit had something to say to us, so I listened, asking Him to show me, and this is what I am hearing and sharing with you.

First morning appearance of the concept: I was reading *Jesus Calling* (2011), and it said this: "I am nearer than you think, richly present in all your moments . . . ask Me to open your eyes, so that you can find Me everywhere. The more aware you are of My presence, the safer you feel. This is not some sort of escape from reality; it is tuning in to *ultimate reality*." The scripture that followed came from Acts 17: 28, and this is what really captured my heart and mind: "For in Him we live and move and have our being."

Live . . . move . . . have our being. What does that really mean? What does that look like today and every day, at work, at home, in the grocery store? **What does that *mean*?** As I pondered this question, a song slipped quietly into my brain. An old song, I think, and in fact, I had to Google the words to get it right:

"I've seen it in the lightning, heard it in the thunder, and felt it in the rain.

My Lord is near me all the time; my Lord is near me all the time."

Wow, omnipresence . . . The song resonated with me because here in Conway, SC, we've had a week of mighty powerful lightning, thunder that sent my sweet dog, Belle, into hiding, and rain

. . . hard, driving rain and soft showers. This morning it's not raining yet, but it's coming; I'm sure it's coming, and in the coming, I will once again think of God's presence: He is here. He is in every part of nature --- in every flower that blooms, in every tree that towers and provides shade, in every cloud in the sky: He is here, near us all the time, *omnipresent.* Can you close your eyes and feel Him with you? Do it: stop right now, close your eyes, and ask Him to help you feel Him all around you. If you need inspiration, look at nature; it's impossible to miss Him out there.

But back to the question: what does it mean to live and move and have our being in God? Well, I think it looks something like this.

Live: when we live "in Him," living looks different than it looks in the world around us. It means we live in grace, freely offered by a God who gave His only Son to provide a grace-filled earthly life and a heavenly eternal life. It means we live in freedom --- freedom from slavery to sin and bondage to condemnation. Oh, yes, we still sin because we are flawed human beings, but we no longer have to be *slaves* to sin. In the words of a wonderful song, "My chains are gone…" And they are. Living in Him also means we live in a spirit of expectation. God has promised to do great things *for* us and *through* us, and believing in that covenant means we can expect God to be *with* us, to answer prayers for us, and to work through us. We live *in Him*.

Move: how do we *move* in Him? Well, we move in ways that Jesus called us to move: we move in love, loving God first, and then loving others as ourselves. We move in grace, paying grace forward to others because God first gave it to us. We move in commitment to Him, understanding our ultimate purpose: to serve and glorify Him all our days. We move, knowing that God has a plan to be accomplished both in us and through us, a plan that He has promised to complete in us until the day of Jesus' second coming. We move in assurance, knowing that He is omnipresent and we are never alone. We move in forgiveness, living free from guilt and forgiving others, no matter what they might have done to us. (It's a mandate and a topic for another writing!) We move boldly at times, proclaiming His goodness to people around us, and we move quietly at other times, reaching out gently and tenderly because the world desperately needs some tenderness. We move like the ultimate example: Christ. He journeyed, He healed, He shook the establishment, but always He moved: fulfilling His earthly calling from His Father, and we are to do the same.

Have our being: that particular phrase boggled me for a moment, but when I searched another Bible, I found the word *exist,* and so I need to be an English teacher for a moment. ☺ *Exist* comes from the French word *exister* and from the Latin *existere*, which means "to step out, to stand forth, to emerge, to appear, to be." So run with me here. We have our being in Him and for Him that we might step out for His glory and His people. We have our being in Him to emerge as His sons and daughters, showing the world to *Whom* we belong. We have our being in Him to spend time in His presence and then stand forth in the world, not losing ourselves in the world's ways and sins. We have our being in Him, simply with the highest privilege of being His children and being co-heirs with His Son, Jesus Christ. We exist because of Him, for Him, and in Him. Without Him, we have nothing and we are nothing. We are His and He is ours, and we move in the world with a sort of holy confidence that comes from having our being in the one who created it all. An humbling thought . . .

So in the coming days as you walk through the journey ahead, start every day with an awareness of God's omnipresence. Whether at home, at a park, in the line at Wal-Mart, or in church --- God is with you. And as you learn to trust in His constant presence, allow Him to wash over you with His love, power, and guidance. When you give yourself over to the Great Creator, the Father of all, you will be able to live, move and have your being, You will be able to walk in joy and peace, no matter the storms that rage in your life or in the lives of others. You will be a positive Christ-walker, following His leading on how to live a faithful life in a challenging, sinful world, and I cannot think of anything better. Live, move and have your being in the omnipresence of God!

Hula Hoop Prayer

I love the book *The Circle Maker* by Mark Batterson, a pastor in Washington, DC. In the book and in the children's book of the same name, he shares the legend of Honi, an "egocentric sage" who believed in the power of prayer in a day and age in which people had wondered if they would ever hear from God again. There was a terrible drought, and the people called upon Honi to pray for rain; he did but in a very unusual way: he drew a circle with a stick, stood inside it, and while on his knees, said this to God: "Lord of the Universe, I swear before Your great name that I will not move from this circle until You have shown mercy upon Your children." Wow, what a bold, gutsy prayer. I get it and I want to be a Honi.

There are some things on my heart these days that have caused me to get more serious than ever about my prayer life; I am taking my cues from Honi, but instead of drawing a circle, I began sitting inside an old broken, blue hula hoop. Okay, I know . . . sounds silly, but for me, it became my way of staying in the circle and praying for answers. Since then I have begun to write the names of people on my prayer list inside circles in my journal. Same idea with a different look. Sometimes I envision myself walking circles around their houses while I pray, and most recently I have taken my prayers for these same people to a new place: I close my eyes and imagine seeing them in a big circle on the ground before the throne of God. Might seem silly to you, but for a visual person like me, this is important. I need to *see* it.

In Batterson's book, he writes this: "The earth has circled the sun more than two thousand times since the day Honi drew his circle in the sand, but God is still looking for circle makers. And the timeless truth secreted within this ancient legend is as true now as it was then: Bold prayers honor God, and God honors bold prayers. He is offended by anything less." I don't ever want to offend God. I want to be accused of being a circle maker and found guilty, and so, I will continue to draw circles in the sand, stand in the circles, and pray boldly for God to act.

Don't misunderstand: I'm not trying to push God around. That's not possible. And I'm not trying to ask for anything that is not in His will. That would be a mistake. But what I am doing is asking for God's mighty hand of protection and strength in some situations. I'm asking for Him to do what seems to be impossible in another situation. I'm asking for every person who is positioned in the circle to be drawn close to Jesus, and that, my friends, is always God's will.

Who needs you to stand in the circle on his or her behalf? Is it a friend? A colleague? A spouse? A pastor? Your community? Your country? Is it you? Are you willing to stand in the circle and pray boldly as Honi did, asking expectantly for God to intervene? And also, are you willing to stand against Satan, dismissing him boldly from those same lives and situations? It's all about bold, audacious, tenacious prayers being lifted to a Sovereign God who loves us and is for us. I don't know about you, but just that knowledge gives me confidence as I lift my hula hoop prayers to heaven.

Dear, God, I'm praying for situations and people, that *You* would be glorified, and I'm standing firm in the circle until I see Your mercy. Praise You, God, for being a Father who sees and hears us!

Jean B. Burden

Not Naturally Equipped

We're in the middle of a deluge of rain, and true to my nature, I decided to sit on the porch for a bit to enjoy the moment. In the midst of a relentless downpour, I watched the birds flying back and forth across my backyard . . . from tree to tree, from tree to feeder, and on to another tree. And in the midst of my watching them, it occurred to me: God was so intentional in the details when He created them to withstand the rain, no matter how heavy. The rain pours off their backs, and they are able to eat and fly, remaining oblivious to the storm around them. Why can't *we* do that?

I have had some storms raging around me in recent days, and of course, I have prayed. But then the other things creep in . . . that thing called worry. . . that thing called anxiety . . . that thing called . . . , well, Satan. He tries to destroy my peace, as he did yesterday at church, because when he throws his flaming arrows and I cower in fear, I lose my focus on the only solution: Jesus. Scripture tells us that Satan prowls like a roaring lion, seeking someone to devour, and one of the mistakes I believe we make as Christians is to behave like he doesn't exist. News flash: he most certainly *does* exist, and he is active and busy, gathering Intel on YOU and ME, Intel that he can use to crush our spirits and send us spiraling away from God. You see, he knows something that the Holy Spirit spoke into my heart this morning: I don't have the capability to let crises and pain pour off my back while I go happily on my way, and neither do you, but we have something infinitely better. We have the promises of God. He promises us in Ephesians that, if we will put on His full armor, we can withstand the fiery missiles of Satan. He also promises us that when we are at our weakest, He is strong. And finally, He promises us that when we are drowning in the deluge of life's trials and tribulations, He will lift us up, set our feet upon the Rock, and help us, in the words of a favorite song, to keep our eyes above the waves. *We* can't do it. *He* can, and *He* will. Just put your eyes, not on the rain, but on Him.

Final advice: every piece of God's armor is urgent, but sometimes the pieces I need the most are the Sword of the Spirit --- His Word--- and prayer. So today, I am fighting back with God's Word. I am recalling His promises to take my impossible situations and create possibilities I cannot even envision. I am reminding myself that as a Christian, I must behave differently than others around me, no matter what they do, because I am *in* the world, not *of* the world. And most importantly, I am choosing to pray. I don't need feathers that repel water because I have the power of prayer and the power of the blood of a Savior. Rain? Oh, yes, it is still raining, but now, it's rolling off my back, and it feels good. Very good. ☺

Living With a Fixer

I live with a "fixer." He can build and fix almost anything… except my car! Dan can repair and install wiring in a home; he can build a room, a house, or a child's toy, and he can build a stable financial future. He also makes a pretty mean Southern meal, which helps to balance my inadequacy! Living with Dan gives me hope for our future because there's not much he can't do around our Boggy Road home and property. But as good as he is, sometimes he fails or I get my feelings hurt, and one day, he won't be here anymore. So as much as he gives me hope, he CANNOT be my ultimate hope; that MUST come from God and God alone.

There are many references to hope in scripture, and we can stand on God's Word in order to have true, lasting, living hope as we walk through our days, each one fraught with valleys and mountaintops. So how does this hope look different from human hope? Let's take a look at the multitude of promises found in His Word.

Psalm 31:24 - Be **strong and courageous**, all you who put your hope in the LORD.

Psalm 33:20-22 - We wait for Yahweh;
He is our **help and shield.**
[21] For our hearts rejoice in Him

because we trust in His holy name.
²² May Your **faithful love** rest on us, Yahweh,
for we put our hope in You.

Psalm 147:11 - The Lord **values those** who fear Him,
those who put their hope in His faithful love.

Hebrews 6:19 - We have this hope as **an anchor** for our lives, **safe and secure**. It enters the inner sanctuary behind the curtain.

Hebrews 10:23 - Let us hold on to the confession of our hope without wavering, for He who promised is **faithful.**

Psalm 46:1 - God is our **refuge and strength**, a **helper** who is **always found** in times of trouble.

Isaiah 40:31 - …but those who trust in the Lord will **renew their strength**;
they will **soar** on wings like eagles;
they will **run** and **not grow weary;**
they will walk and not faint.

Jeremiah 29:11 – "For I know the plans I have for you"— this is **the Lord's declaration**—"plans for your welfare, not for disaster, **to give you a future and a hope."**

So let's piece together these images of who God can be when we put our hope in Him --- our help, our shield, our faithful Father, our anchor that creates safety and security, our refuge and strength, our helper, and the one who values us.

And what can *we* be when we put our hope in Him? Strong and courageous, full of rejoicing, safe and secure, never alone in times of trouble, able to soar, run and walk without growing weary . . . and finally? We get to have a future filled with God's plans, plans for our welfare, and not for disaster. A future and a hope because we have chosen to trust in Him.

On the contrary, what does the world offer us? Oh, it offers hope, sometimes through a job, an opportunity, or a relationship. But jobs are lost, opportunities don't always pan out the way we want, and relationships fail. And Satan offers us hope through sin . . . the sins of addiction, adultery, covetousness . . . all sins that make us feel hopeful for a moment but never for a lifetime.

Do you want *real* hope? *Lasting* hope? Hope that *never disappoints*? Put your hope in God, wait for Him, trust Him, and look with hope to your future, one filled with plans and dreams bigger than you can even imagine. Do I live with hope, even in the midst of the valleys of my life? I surely do ---every single day --- because God has proven Himself faithful, and it doesn't get more hopeful than this.

Missing the Truths

I am, in both great and terrible ways, a product of childhood Sunday School. My parents were faithful to take me to church from the time I was born, and I don't think I ever missed Sunday morning classes as a child. But I've realized something in the last few years: as wonderful as those times were and as many stories as I learned, I somehow learned the stories themselves without the truths of God's Word attached. Maybe I was too interested in the action of the story itself to hook into the truth. (I love a great action and adventure story!) Maybe I heard those lessons but forgot them along the way. However it happened, I learned the stories but lost the urgent truths, and today as I studied a well-written lesson about Jonah, I was reminded of the power in the lessons embedded in those awesome stories.

There are quite a few powerful lessons from the story of Jonah, a prophet sent by God to proclaim a simple message of impending doom and God's grace. I want to give you a simple list of what the Holy Spirit showed me this morning, and then I'll camp on one particular lesson that is especially urgent for our times.

Lesson # 1: God was indeed pursuing the Ninevites, but in that process He had to pursue Jonah as well. Jonah's disobedience to God's call required grace, and the same is true of us today.

Lesson #2: When the men on the ship threw Jonah overboard, having realized that he was the cause of the mighty storm, God was able to show Himself to the men on the ship as well, and they ended up making vows to Him. Wonderful thing about God: He can create collateral goodness when He is going about reaching people.

Lesson #3: God spoke to His Creation twice in this story, and Creation obeyed! He calmed the raging sea, and He told the great fish to spit Jonah out. God is omnipotent and has the power to do anything and everything!

Lesson #4: God can do mighty acts through simple messages when we are obedient to His calling on our lives. Jonah's message was very, very simple: "Yet forty days and Ninevah shall be overthrown!" That's it. Warning! Nothing else but a simple, clean message of truth, and God used it to save a huge city of people who heeded the warning, called for a fast, put on sackcloth, and repented.

Lesson #5: This is the big one: Jonah was not able to be happy for the redemption of his enemies. Are we so different?

This is the hard truth . . . "The sad story of Jonah reveals how deeply we can resent other people. We draw lines based on culture, race, disease, and background, and those lines cause us to be disobedient to God's plan."

In this particular story, everyone deserved to be punished:

the Ninevites, Jonah, and even the men on the ship who had been worshiping other gods. But we serve a God who is full of mercy, grace, and compassion, and is only satisfied when we recognize Him as the one true God. In the story, Jonah was finally willing to share the message of God's impending punishment, but somehow, he could not bring himself to rejoice for his enemies. I'm afraid we are way too often in the same "boat" as Jonah.

In the words of this lesson, we "distance ourselves" from people God loves . . . people of other races, other backgrounds, other financial statuses, but God loves EVERYONE. Yes, He loves you and He loves me, but He also loves every single person on this planet. My worry for us today is that we are not confronting the heart issues that God is asking us to recognize and allow Him to change. Just like Jonah, we are often "clinging to the idols of [our] own hatred," "recognizing the magnitude of God's gracious compassion," but not able to be compassionate for others ourselves. But God is calling *all of us* to repent.

He is calling us, as Christians, to be a beacon of love and hope for all people . . . even our "enemies." Maybe you are saying to yourself, "But I don't have any enemies." I would argue that maybe you do. Do you hang onto negative images of other races?

Negative images of people in society who disagree with you?

Negative images of people who argue a strong political platform other than yours?

Negative images of people who, in your opinion, are lazy and taking advantage of the system? Negative images of people who have made terrible mistakes, either privately or publicly?

But God says we must have compassion . . . and we don't get to decide who gets His measure of love and grace.

God says that we must love people and do something meaningful with that love.

God says that we must be obedient to *His* call, even when it is with those we consider to be our enemies.

You see, God's call is not always easy. It can't always be done with an e-mail or phone call. Sometimes we have to travel to the very places we dread and share God's message of hope and love. And how does that look? I don't know what it looks like for you. Each one of us must be in relationship with God and must ask Him: "What is it You are calling *me* to do? Where is my Ninevah?" And then? We must go where He tells us to go and do what He instructs us to do. Obedience is not always easy but it is the urgent truth of living in relationship with God. He is our Father and He expects us to listen and obey. After all, He knows what a difference even one person can make . . . one person who follows His call.

So "How will your story end? Will you sit on the hill of disobedience, or will you rejoice in and share of the gracious character of God in Christ?" Today I will surely examine my heart once again and say to God, "Here I am, Lord; send me." I pray you will do the same, but before you do, get ready: God will bless you in your obedience, and He just might blow you away with His goodness. ☺

(Excerpts taken from *The Gospel Project*, Volume 5, Lifeway Press, pages 74-81).

Okay? Stop Asking and Be Decisive!

It was the summer of 1979, and I was a student intern in Charlotte, NC. I was serving in a school for students with serious emotional difficulties, and my observer, Ms. Helen Abell, would visit and watch me teach. In one situation she was able to sit behind one-way glass and observe my work. In a particularly memorable conference, she shared something she noticed about me: every time I asked students to do something, I would end my request with, "Okay?" Hmm . . . are you asking them if they are willing to do the work? Are you being wishy-washy about your assignment? Ending with that one-word question made my requirement sound like an option. I never even realized I was saying it so often, but the impact of the questioning word was clear: are you okay with doing what I asked? It's not what I meant to do, but it was the message I was sending.

Do we send that message when we tell others about life in Christ? Do we say "You need to follow Jesus, okay?" Or do we say, "Jesus loves you unconditionally and He is the ***only way*** to heaven. I pray you will follow Him." The two messages are *not* the same: one sounds wimpy and optional, but the latter is strong and sure.

We need Christians who are being strong and sure about the message of Christ's love and our futures. In John 14: 16, we read these words of Jesus: "Jesus told him, 'I am **the way, the truth,** and **the** life. No one comes to the Father except **through Me**.'" Nothing wimpy about those words, and they leave no room for wonder or questioning. In other passages, Jesus calls Himself the door . . . the *only* door to eternal life. He doesn't ask us if it's okay with us; He gives us the Truth of His Word, and yes, He lets us choose, but He never suggests even once that without Him, we will be okay.

We won't.

Jesus made choices on our behalf. He chose to leave Heaven and come to earth as a man. He chose to live a sinless life. He chose to reject the status quo, knowing what His choices would cause. He chose to love people in ways never seen before. He chose to die . . . to allow Himself to be arrested, beaten, and nailed to a Cross in the most horrific of deaths. And then? He chose to accept the weight of our sins on His shoulders. He took everything we deserved and sacrificed Himself, all because God knew we needed a blood sacrifice ---a sacrificial, perfect Lamb --- to pay the penalty for our sinful selves.

It's hard to understand how He could do so much for us, but it's summed up in one word: love. He doesn't say, "I love you, okay?" He says, "I love you, and I died for you." Period. No need for a comma here because the period is in place; He took care of it once and for all. We are no longer guilty, and because of His sacrifice, we have been able to become the righteousness of God.

A pretty solid gift, don't you think? There's nothing to wonder or question. Nothing that deserves our tiptoeing around His offer, saying to unbelievers, "He's a pretty good Savior, okay?" He is an amazing Savior and a faithful friend, and when He left us to return to Heaven, He gave us a tremendous gift: the gift of the Holy Spirit, left to reside within our hearts and souls. It's hard to comprehend that anything could be better than Jesus, but the Holy Spirit does something for us that only He can do: He is in us, with us, and working for us, sharing the very things He hears from God for our lives. And once again, there's nothing shaky or indecisive about that.

I don't know where you are in your faith journey, so I want to leave you with this: Jesus is the only way --- our High Priest who sits at the right hand of God. God is the only God --- the Sovereign Father who knows all, loves, all, and desires peace for us. The Holy Spirit is our only Advocate – the one who walks with us and guides us every single day. Don't fool yourself and think that there might be a substitute: there is not. And if you are only hearing this Good News with an "Okay?" question at the end, you will miss it all.

Please don't see following Jesus as an option; instead of "Okay," say to Him, "Yes! Okay! You are my only Savior!"

And then? Life will be more than okay. ☺

Who's Your Daddy?

I saw the most disturbing billboard recently. Its slogan said, "Who's your daddy?" and it was advertising DNA testing. Wow. So sad that we live in a world in which we have given ourselves away to the point that we can't identify the daddy of our children. We need a DNA test to confirm fatherhood, and this new technology is amazing, but the reality of this particular use is so sad.

But here's what I began to celebrate in that moment of clarity: there may be women in the world who can't name the father of their baby, but we all have a Father we can name: God. We don't need a DNA test to be sure we are His because His Word is clear. He adopted us as His children, and we will forever be a part of the family of God.

No need to wonder, and yet, people still do. So what does Scripture say about our paternity?

In **Psalm 68: 5**, we find these words:

"God in His holy dwelling is a father of the fatherless and a champion of widows."

In other words, we are never orphans or lonely widows as long as we know God, father of the fatherless.

And then in **Matthew 23: 9,** it says this: "Do not call anyone on earth your father, because you have one Father, who is in heaven. This surely is good news for all, but especially for those whose earthly father is absent."

And there's more, **Ephesians 4: 4-6**, is another assurance of our heavenly paternity:

"There is one body and one Spirit—just as you were called to one hope at your calling—one Lord, one faith, one baptism, one God and Father of all, who is above all and through all and in all."

More good news . . . he's not just our Father, but He is the same Father for all of us.

Isaiah 64: 8, is one of my personal favorites: "Yet LORD, YOU ARE OUR FATHER; we are the clay, and You are our potter; we all are the work of Your hands."

That's such a beautiful image of God, our Father and Maker. We are the clay on His wheel, and He is our Potter, having made us exactly as He chose. He is Potter and Father, and we are molded in His image as His children.

And finally, in **1 Corinthians 8:6**, we find this assurance:

Yet for us there is one God, the Father.
All things are from Him,
and we exist for Him.
And there is one Lord, Jesus Christ.
All things are through Him,
and we exist through Him.

Life can leave us with questions and doubts, but there is no doubt about our heavenly paternity: scripture is clear and true. In fact, in Mark 14: 36, Jesus calls God, "Abba, Father." God is our Father, our Champion, our hope, and our Potter. We exist for Him and through Him, and we, as His children, are from Him.

No DNA test needed here. Today I urge you to see yourself as His son or daughter, confident in the fact that the Maker of the Universe in indeed your Daddy!

Just An Ordinary Little Girl

She was an ordinary little girl. She "cooed" on time. She walked on time. She spoke words on time.

>Just nicely ordinary.

When she started school, she saw other boys and girls, and she thought:

>I'm just ordinary . . . nothing special.

Sarah can jump higher then I can. John runs faster . . . Mya is prettier.

And when she compared herself to others, she always felt plain and ordinary.

But one day, she heard a story of an ordinary baby. His name was Jesus. He was born in an ordinary stable with ordinary animals watching the birth.

He grew into a young boy, living an ordinary life as the son of a carpenter.

But then, He began to look anything *but* ordinary.

He became the **kindest** man ever to live. He became the **best teacher** ever to teach. He taught **new lessons** that changed the world --- lessons about love and compassion and forgiveness.

And this Jesus? He loved children . . . *ALL* of them. In His eyes, they were *not* ordinary. They were beautiful and special!

Jesus lived in an age, a long time ago, when women were not honored and respected . . . they felt less than ordinary. But Jesus included women as His friends and disciples.

You see, He knew they were anything but ordinary.

And that's what He knows about you, too!

God made every one of His children with special, **extra**-ordinary gifts and talents.

And that means you!

He made you to be a unique, extraordinary person --- fearfully and wonderfully made.

And just like Diana Prince, AKA Wonder Woman, becomes an extraordinary superhero when she puts on her costume, we must put on the *most* important gifts given from God so we can be anything-but-ordinary Super Heroes in His Kingdom and in our world today.

We can go from ordinary to Super . . . from ordinary to Wonderful . . . from ordinary to Extraordinary!

So when you look at yourself, be joyful that God gave you just the right super powers to be the person He designed you to be...

Super powers of kindness, and love, and knowledge, and intelligence.

Super powers of listening, and caring, and sharing, and trusting.

Super powers of laughter and confidence, and creating and shaping.

And most of all, the super power of knowing you are *His* child... perfectly made in *His* image!

Just exactly unique and NOT ordinary at all!

And when God gives you these anything-but-ordinary gifts, He expects you to use them to change the world for good.

And THAT, my sweet friends, is NOT ordinary!

So this Grandma's call to you today is this:

Believe in who God created you to be... an extraordinary daughter or son of the King of the World!

And each day, put on your cape and your crown, and know that every single person you meet is NOT ordinary but extraordinary in ways that only God can create, and part of your destiny is to use your powers to help them see their greatness... just like God sees the greatness in you!

This is dedicated to my extraordinary children and grandchildren, to be shared with every extraordinary woman, man, and child.

Jeremiah 1:5 - "Before I formed you in the womb I knew you, before you were born I set you apart; I appointed you as a prophet to the nations."

Psalm 139:14 – "I praise you because I have been remarkably and wonderfully made. Your works are wonderful, and I know this very well."

Top Ten for Today

Some things I know this morning . . . maybe you know these, too, or just maybe you need a reminder:

1) God's Word is as relevant today as it was when it was written. If you don't get that, you haven't been reading it.

2) If we really want God to be "in our business" every single day, then all we have to do is ask. He is waiting to involve Himself in our lives, minute by minute.

3) If you are not spending time with Him, don't expect to know Him. Make time to study and pray. Everything else must fall away until this is in place.

4) God answers in the most creative ways. I constantly ask Him to enlarge my territory for Him, and most times, He does it in a way I couldn't see coming. I love His surprises!

5) Forgiveness is non-negotiable. If you keep saying you just can't forgive, then expect not to have peace or be forgiven. BIG TRUTH: if Jesus can forgive us for all the junk we have

done, how dare we not forgive others for what they have done to us!

6) Worship of God must be both corporate and personal. If you can't make time to worship Him in private and worship with others, then you simply are not doing what God commanded. Period.

7) God asks us . . . in His Word . . . not to grumble and complain about anything, but in everything, pray. Some of the stuff I read on Facebook goes directly against His Word. Guess what . . . He can see FB, too.

8) You and I do not have to know "why" about everything. God is simply smarter than we are, and He has a bigger picture in mind. Don't spend your days trying to figure everything out. Just trust Him.

9) If you have quit going to church because you think there are hypocrites there, well guess what: we are ALL sinners. Nowhere in scripture does it say that once you join a church, you stop sinning. That's why we need grace. But being in a church where there are people seeking God, even through their failures, provides fellowship, strength, and prayer warriors to lift you up and help you grow.

10) I believe that America is in a mess today because so many people have moved to "God-light." They don't want to study, be faithful, live by God's Word when it is hard, or change for the sake of being who God designed us to be; this life of faith is not always easy, but it is so worth it. As a nation, we have compromised our values, and we are paying dearly.

Christians, live by what you say you believe. Dedicate yourselves and your lives to knowing God, your Father, and living by His commands. Stop compromising. Jesus didn't compromise a single time, and He is our role model.

When Life Gets Top-Heavy

Sometimes we create a situation that is destined to crash and burn. For instance, this morning I was tending to my indoor plants. Three of them have a wonderful clay watering system that utilizes a big bottle turned upside down; the bottle drips water into the clay funnel to meet each plant's needs. For no purpose at all, I switched two of the bottles after filling them with water. As I put the last one in place, I sensed that it felt a little unstable, but I left it there anyway. Careless, foolish mistake. Within just a few minutes, the top-heavy bottle forced my ponytail fern to the floor, dumping dirt and water in a three-foot circle. A huge mess to clean, and it gave me a word: sometimes we allow things in life to get top-heavy, and eventually, they will always crash to the ground.

When I speak of being top-heavy, I am thinking about how we, as logical human beings, want to think our way through everything, using the brain given to us by our good God. However, God did not intend us to live in brain-mode all the time, especially where He is concerned. You see, God needs us to live in heart-mode and faith-mode, the place where the Holy Spirit can guide and speak, and when we don't allow His still small voice to be heard, we stay in our heads, and yes, things often crash and burn.

So let's follow this analogy a little further. When my flower pot crashed this morning, dirt went everywhere. It splattered on the baseboards and sent water trickling across the tile floor, creating unwanted mud pies in my house. And isn't life like that when we make careless decisions? We are reasoning our way through life, and when things crash, there is always collateral damage. Just like the dirt and water that made a filthy mess, our top-heavy choices can have ripple effects in our lives and the lives of others. Example . . . we decide to take on a job God never intended us to do, and our stress level goes haywire while our families suffer. Collateral damage. Or we volunteer for a project that was not ours to complete, and in the process, we keep another servant from stepping up and growing by being the hands and feet of Christ. Collateral damage. Or my recent situation, we are tempted to stay in a position too long, after its season is over in our lives, but we just can't let go. We find ourselves exhausted and unhappy. Collateral damage.

Recently in my own life, I have been struggling with a big decision. I pray and I commit my decision to God, but then my head comes along and interferes. I begin to rationalize why this or that doesn't make sense . . . isn't logical . . . isn't financially sound. And yet, in my experience with God, He often calls me to things that are not logical and don't make sense in the practical realm. When I listen with my heart and my spirit, He pushes me to make choices that are radical, a little frightening and life-changing.

So what does this require of me? Trust.

Complete trust in an omniscient God, who has my whole life mapped out in a perfect blueprint if I will only follow. In the words of scripture, I must seek Him and He will be found. Seek Him before the answers, before the decisions . . . just seek Him, and then He will surely guide us into His perfect plan for our lives. Let me leave you with a favorite poem, "The Weaver," (Anonymous) that I often use when teaching because its images are powerful and true...

Jean B. Burden

My life is but a weaving, between my God and me,
I do not choose the colors, He worketh steadily.
Ofttimes he weaveth sorrow, and I in foolish pride
Forget He sees the upper, and I the underside.
Not till the loom is silent, and the shuttles cease to fly,
Will God unroll the canvas, and explain the reasons why
The dark threads are as needful in the skillful weaver's hand
As threads of gold and silver in the pattern He has planned.

He knows, He loves, He cares,
Nothing this truth can dim.
He gives His very best to those
Who leave the choice with Him.

The World's Confusion

I was in a dentist's office last summer with my son as we waited for him to have some dental surgery. As we waited . . . and waited and waited and waited . . . I noticed an odd advertisement on a vending machine: "Good for you!" After reading the logo, I began to look at the offerings in the machine, thinking that if they are using those words, there must be some healthy options. But no, I found the usual unhealthy suspects: crackers, candy bars, honey buns, and other choices that definitely are NOT good for you. So I began to think about this --- how often does the world offer us ideas, products, beliefs, or lifestyles with the heading "Good for you" when in fact they are just the opposite? Let's ponder this for a minute, looking at examples and evaluating what they really offer.

First example: Happy Hour! It's good for you, right? You save money and you hang out with friends. But good for you? No. The Bible is clear that drunkenness is a problem, and I've watched alcohol abuse destroy families. Not so good. And there's more . . . what about going in debt to have the material things the world tells us we deserve? Buy that house that's bigger than what you need, buy that boat that will leave you in debt, buy . . . well, whatever it is that is more than we need and keeps us from what's truly important. Anything that becomes so important to us that we lose all logic and allow material possessions to become an idol is a serious problem. Owning things is perfectly okay, but when those things take center stage, they surely are not good for us. And there are so many other examples . . . relationships outside of marriage, gluttony at the all-you-can-eat buffet, drugs that mask our troubles . . . all of these would tell us, "Good for you!" But they certainly are not, so why do we allow false advertising to sway us when we know better? Well, there's a reason.

God's word is clear, all the way back to the Ten Commandments: let no idol com before Him. And yet, humans continue to be drawn away from putting Him first, wooed by the idea that things out in the world are good for us when they are not. This happens because we lost sight of two things: first, we forget to keep our eyes on God and our hearts seeking *His* will for us, not our wills. Second, we easily forget that there is an enemy in the world who is seeking to kill, steal, and destroy our lives. Some Bible translations use the word "devour" and that's an image that should wake us up from our confusion about what's good for us and what's actually harmful. Satan will use anything to destroy us and our relationship with God. If he can get us to value things above God, he wins, even if just temporarily. If he can get us to believe lies, he wins. If he can keep us from recognizing that he is at work around us, trying to devour us, he wins. If he can convince us to live in fear instead of faith, he wins. So why do we let him win when we know his plans are never good for us? Let me share a conversation I had just recently with one of my sons.

We were talking about God and how the world tried for years to draw him away from the truth he was taught as a child. But then he began to read and study for himself, and he returned to the truth: God is sovereign and good; Satan is real and evil. The end. We lose sight of this when we have silly images of Satan as a red devil with horns and a tail, but that's not an accurate picture. That's a silly Halloween image, and if this is the way we see him, we have already begun to lose. Satan is our enemy, an angel who was thrown out of heaven because of his ego-filled heart: he wanted to be bigger than God. And even worse, he has legions with him, hovering in our world, carrying out evil plans directly aimed at our hearts. He knows enough about each one of us to use the very thing that will take us down, *if* we fall prey to his schemes. He knows my Achilles heel and yours, and he uses our weaknesses to confuse us and convince us that his lies are the truth. He is a liar, a schemer, and a destroyer, and yet, we don't have to let him win. There's victory and hope found in Jesus.

Read these words found in 1 Peter 5: "Humble yourselves, therefore, under God's mighty hand, that He may lift you up in due time. Cast all your anxiety on Him because He cares for you. Be alert and of sober mind. Your enemy the devil prowls around like a roaring lion looking for someone to devour. Resist him, standing firm in the faith, because you know that the family of believers throughout the world is undergoing the same kind of sufferings. And the God of all grace, who called you to His eternal glory in Christ, after you have suffered a little while, will himself restore you and make you strong, firm and steadfast. To Him be the power forever and ever. Amen."

So let's take this apart just a little: first, we must always be humble before God, realizing that in ourselves, we don't have the strength, power, or mind to resist trouble. Second, we need to cast our problems and cares on Him. He loves us and He is able to handle them all. Third, we must resist Satan, seeking guidance for every decision and question about what's good and right for us. Fourth, we must know with confidence that He will make us strong, firm and steadfast . . . able to stand against Satan's lies and attacks. And is this good for us? Oh, yes, it is. God is Father, and He will always guide us to the very things that are truly good for us.

Today, trust God and His sovereign knowledge of what is good for you in a world full of temptations claiming goodness and leaving us in dangerous places. In the world, you will find paradoxes of lies clothed to look like truth, but with God, truth is clear and perfect. Sounds like a life that is truly "good for you!" ☺

He Was a Good, Good Father:
A Daughter's Lessons about Fatherhood from a Man Who Did It Right

I sat in church this morning and listened to the sweet voices of children singing, "You're a good, good Father, that's who You are." (Chris Tomlin) I know they were singing about God, but their song made me think about my earthly father, and yes, he was very good. So indulge me as I share what he did right that maybe someone who reads this --- some sweet new father or a discouraged, tired father --- needs to hear. Put these on your refrigerator and in your heart; he's worth following.

1. My daddy was a good father because he loved God first. I remember watching him walking down the aisle of First Baptist Church, Walterboro, serving as a deacon, serving Communion, and serving God. He kept Sunday School records and cooked for church events, and he was faithful in his attendance. But even more than all of this, he lived out his life, loving people the way Christ expected him to do, and I watched everything.

2. He was a good father because he loved our mother, right to the very end of her life. He cooked *for* her and *with* her; he allowed her to sleep late while

he washed the clothes and hung them on the line in the yard; he canned vegetables and made fruit cake at Christmas, all right beside our mom, in their tiny crowded kitchen. And when cancer entered the picture, he stood firmly beside her, loving her all the way. She was the love of his life, and it showed in everything he did. I loved him even more because he loved my beautiful mother right in front of my eyes.

3. He was a good father because I watched him love *his* mother. Until she died at 96 years old, he cared for her, visited her every single day and sometimes twice a day, helped her with flowers, and watched Braves baseball in her tiny den. Even when he met a sweet woman years after my mother died and he cared very deeply for her, their relationship ended because she lived in another town and neither would desert their mothers. I watched and learned about family commitment from my father.

4. He was an incredible father to three girls, even though he was the epitome of an outdoors, hunting and fishing kind of guy. He took us clothes shopping and shoe shopping every August before school started. He went to every cheerleading event, every long piano recital, and every high school concert in which I participated. I'm sure he would have loved to have a son who would hunt and fish with him, but I never knew it. Later in our adult relationship, I told him to stop giving me pocketbooks and blue jeans for Christmas; I wanted something *he* loved so we

could share it, and this began my hobby of collecting knives. Only Case knives because that's what he loved. I have quite a collection today, and when I hold them, I think of him.

5. He was a good role model because he respected and loved nature. He hunted and fished but only for food for our family --- never for the kill. He and his mother, Belle, grew the most amazing flowers in their backyards, and they passed this love of God's beauties to me. When he was offered a good bit of money from an oil company to drill his five acres of land in Lodge, SC, he said, "Absolutely not." You see, he had planted fruit trees, and he couldn't bear seeing them destroyed for the sake of a dollar. Yes, he loved nature, and I relish in it today because he modeled it all his life.

6. He was a good father because he was a hard worker. My father was an insurance salesman, and he worked hard to meet the expectations of his company, but he did it in a way that oozed with integrity. When a family was struggling to pay an insurance premium, he paid it. When he visited his clients to pick up monthly premiums, he stayed to talk, showing true friendship rather than just a business relationship. Being the outdoorsman he was, he loved to go fishing every Thursday, and to make up for that time of pleasure, he worked late two nights a week. In a day when integrity is missing everywhere, he was a model of honesty and a strong work ethic. I am the

hard worker I am today, partially because I watched him in action.

7. He was a good father because he lived with joy. My daddy woke up happy and remained happy throughout his day, no matter what he was doing. He truly lived with the joy of the Lord, never complaining that I remember, and he had a constant smile on his face. After I moved to Conway, I would visit with my family, and he would always take us to Hardee's to get a sandwich. The clerks' responses to him told a story without words: they loved seeing him walk in the door, calling him "Mr. Murry" and returning the smiles he freely gave. My father created joy everywhere he went, whether to church, to the grocery story, or at home. It wasn't fake; it wasn't forced; it was the real deal, and I am incredibly grateful that I inherited his joyful spirit.

8. In the Bible, Jesus spoke clearly about how we are to love others, and my father took that mandate seriously. In Matthew 25:35-36, the scripture says this:
For I was hungry and you gave Me something to eat;
I was thirsty and you gave Me something to drink;
I was a stranger and you took Me in;
I was naked and you clothed Me;
I was sick and you took care of Me;
I was in prison and you visited Me.

My daddy was a good, good father because he loved

others in a real way . . . in the way Jesus demanded. He shared with people in need, whether it was a bag of garden vegetables or help with insurance. When our mother was diagnosed with cancer, he took care of her. I remember clearly the day he called me at work and said, "Baby, I can't do this anymore. Her pain is too severe, and I need help. And I need you to be okay with this." You see, I was about 36 weeks pregnant, and I wanted my momma to stay at home until that sweet baby was born. He tried his best to make it happen, taking care of her with love and dignity until what he could offer was not enough. After that conversation, he took her to the hospital, and she never came home again, but he was by her side every single day, loving her in the way he promised the day he married her . . . until death they parted. That was real for him, and he never would have considered being anywhere but at her bedside. If that day ever comes in my marriage, he will be my model of how to love to the end and be committed without wavering. He really was a good, good father.

9. My daddy was a good father because he was a sacrificial giver when it came to his children. My parents didn't have a lot of money, but they always made sure I had the best piano lessons, cheerleader uniforms, and more. When I decided to attend Winthrop, they supported that decision. I had a few scholarships, but I never knew until years later that they took out a second mortgage on their house so I could become a

teacher. When I wanted to change teaching areas and needed to take another test (the NTE at that time) but I couldn't afford the fee, he gladly paid it so I could move into elementary education. He and my mother rarely had anything new, and they even shared a single car so I could student teach. They gave sacrificially, and I know without a doubt that they learned it from Christ, the ultimate sacrificial Giver.

10. Finally, my father (and mother) raised me in church. They modeled faithful attendance, making sure we were in the doors for everything. And yes, he even made me behave in church and be quiet! When the preacher called my friends and me out one day for talking during the sermon, my daddy handled it: I had to sit with him for the next few weeks and needless to say, I didn't say a word, but in that lesson, I learned respect for worship, the pastor, and others around me. They took me to youth group, the Girls in Action meetings, and always Sunday School. When I played handbells or the piano in church, they were there to support me and encourage me. When I wanted to go to church music camp, they made that happen. They taught me a level of commitment not always seen in today's world. Did it keep me from straying? No, it did not, and I hate to admit that truth (that's a lesson for another time!), but their dedication to keeping us in church showed me what they valued: God and family. We were grounded in the stories of the Bible . . . we were the picture of what

scripture says: Raise up your children in the way they should go and they will not depart from it. Yes, I departed for a few years, but the solid foundation and God's grace brought me back, and today I love knowing that I am part of a generational legacy of loving the Lord, from my grandparents, to my parents, and now to my children and grandchildren. My good, good Father made sure I knew THE good, good Father, and what a gift it is!

Jean B. Burden

Thanking the Saints

This is a personal statement of thanks, but please take time to read. Let it cause you to think about the "saints" who have lived extraordinary lives and changed your ways of living. And then ask yourself: who are the Saints in your life and what gifts did their presence provide? Who needs a thank you from you?

In November, the Methodist Church celebrates All Saints' Day, and because I didn't grow up in the Methodist tradition, this was a new experience for me in 2015. I loved it! We took time in the morning service to honor those who went to be with the Lord during this past year, and the pastor reminded us that we build upon the foundation these saints laid for us. What a gift! These were ordinary people who reflected the life of Jesus Christ, therefore affecting those around them. Which begs the question: Who are the saints who have affected my life? What have they done that has guided my faith development and molded me into the woman I am today? Who might I need to thank during this season of thanksgiving? I will share mine, and I pray that this will prompt you to ponder and thank yours as well.

Lord, for my Sunday School teachers who taught me Your stories and Your truths . . . I thank You.
Lord, for my pastors -- both past and present – who have

been willing to speak hard truths from the pulpit and in the hallways of life . . . I thank You.

Lord, for the musicians who have stirred my passion for music and taught me the power of song . . . I thank You.

Lord, for my piano teacher and my first chorus director --- they channeled my natural gift of music and created life-long possibilities in me   . . . I thank You.

Lord, for the teachers who loved me first and then held me to a high standard . . . I thank You.

Lord, for my cousin who was a childhood playmate and is now a loving Christian sister . . . I thank You.

Lord, for the people who hurt me and caused me to grow up . . . I thank You.

Lord, for my husband, who found me and married me for the last time . . . I thank You.

Lord, for my children, who have filled my heart and home to overflowing . . . I thank You.

Lord, for my grandchildren, who have filled an empty space in my heart I didn't even know I had . . . I thank You.

Lord, for my father, who loved unconditionally and modeled priorities . . . I thank You.

Lord, for my mother, a woman who loved You and loved me --- my best friend --- I thank You.

Lord, for every rough valley that tested my faith . . . I thank You.

Lord, thank You for these saints, whose lives have created the pieces of the tapestry of my life…still under construction but woven with myriad colors that are the fabric of who I am.

Lord, I thank You for these ordinary people of extraordinary commitment, "men and women made of human flesh with rough edges but transparent to something so extraordinary that ever so often it stops us dead in our tracks. We've had a nice life together." -- Pastor Marie Nuckles

I challenge you today: take a moment to reflect on the saints who changed your life. Commit your list to paper, thank the ones who are still available, and lift prayers of thanksgiving to God for every single name on your list. It's time to thank the Saints, and then pay it forward by being a Saint to the people in your life today who need you as a Christian role model!

Weeds: A Never-Ending Reality

Recently my husband and I bought a daylily farm, and I truly am living the dream! I never imagined that I would be a small business owner, even though I have loved flowers all my life. But when God opens a door and the Holy Spirit tells me to walk through it, I do it without question, and so my days right now are spent in the yard --- AKA: in the heat! --- tending flowers, deadheading yesterday's blooms, fertilizing, and yes, pulling weeds. Weeds, weeds, weeds. They are never-ending. But as I pulled and walked the garden a few days ago, I thought about how this is just like life: life can be as beautiful as the most gorgeous flower, but weeds are always in the picture. Reality check.

As I ponder this idea this morning, I am filled with gratitude for the beauty in my life, and I am sure you can make a long list of things for which you are thankful, too. I have a peaceful home in the country, a loving husband, and a big, noisy family full of children and grandchildren. I am teaching college classes for pre-service teachers and a young adult Sunday School class, both of which I am created to do. I am singing and speaking for God and writing about His goodness --- I could tell you more because I constantly *look* for reasons to be grateful . . . reasons both big and small. But here's the reality check: in the midst of all this goodness and this wealth of blessings, the weeds are there. Growing, infiltrating, sneaking into the garden of my life when I least expect it. And it's happening to you, too.

A couple of months ago, I found myself in one of the worst crises ever with one of my children. It is the kind of thing that knocks you down but also brings you to your knees in prayer. Very soon after this news, more things came against me and my family --- dissension, a car accident, hurt feelings, and concerns for the future. Just before all of this occurred, I had retired from full-time work for the second time, feeling sure I would have plenty of classes to teach at the colleges, but at the time of this writing, they have not materialized. So on top of the family worries, my human nature wants to be a little alarmed about this lack of security I am facing. Weeds . . . insidious, vicious weeds. But guess what: God has given us an arsenal of holy weapons to fight the weeds, our own version of Round Up.

First of all, He told us to expect the weeds so they shouldn't take us by surprise. In John 16:33, we read these words of Jesus: "I have told you these things so that in Me you may have peace. You will have suffering in this world. Be courageous! I have conquered the world." Did you notice what He said? We will experience suffering. Period. But He also said that we can be encouraged because He has overcome the world, and He loves us and is waiting to help us overcome it, too, both while we are here on earth and when we go to our final home in Heaven. Jesus never sugarcoated things in His words; He said that we will face weeds, but we don't have to face them alone. But there's more.

In Philippians 4:6-7, we are told not to worry but to pray. Here's how it reads in *The Message*: "Don't fret or worry. Instead of worrying, pray. Let petitions and praises shape your worries into prayers, letting God know your concerns. Before you know it, a sense of God's wholeness, everything coming together for good, will come and settle you down. It's wonderful what happens when Christ displaces worry at the center of your life."

I love that phrase: *let petitions and praises shape your worries into prayers.* Notice that it says we are to *petition* God and to *praise* Him, even in the midst of the weeds of worry. And then Christ, our Savior, can displace the worry and replace it with peace. We simply don't have to let the weeds make us sick; we have to give them to God and let Him handle them for us. In fact, it says in another place in scripture that we can cast our cares on Him because He cares for us ... just like a good, good, Father. Comforting. But does this mean the weeds will go away? Probably not or at least not right away, so there are more weapons at our disposal.

In Ephesians 6:13-18, we are told to use the powerful, spiritual weapons God has given us. Listen to His Word: "Be prepared. You're up against far more than you can handle on your own. Take all the help you can get, every weapon God has issued, so that when it's all over but the shouting you'll still be on your feet. Truth, righteousness, peace, faith, and salvation are more than words. Learn how to apply them. You'll need them throughout your life. God's Word is an *indispensable* weapon." (MSG) An indispensable weapon.

His Sword of the Spirit, which is the Word of God, cuts down every weed. But to be able to draw upon His Word, we must be prepared by reading it, learning it, and using it as the weed killer it was intended to be.

Will the weeds continue to attack the gardens of our lives? They most surely will. But we don't have to let them win or take over or steal the beauty in our lives. We serve a God who has given us the fertilizer --- His Word --- and weapons --- His Armor --- so we can stand strong with *His* strength, not our own.

News flash: You don't have to do this life alone . . . ever. When life feels perfect, praise Him. When the weeds show up and attempt to devour your life, praise Him and call upon His Word as an offensive weapon against the enemy.

Will I continue to pull weeds in my garden? Oh, yes, I am headed there as soon as I finish this writing, but I take the weeds one day at a time, knowing that they can't defeat me and cannot destroy the beauty of what God has created in my garden and in my life and yours.

I beg you today: don't succumb to the weeds. Call out to friends who will pray for you and with you. Call out to our Sovereign God who is our Father and wants the very best for us. And then? Stand strong in the peace and security of the Father's love, and watch Him handle your weeds!

Petition + praise + prayer = peace

Finding Faith in the Storm

It was just before 1:30 PM on a beautiful July afternoon. I was unloading my car at the Conway Recreation Center for what my family now calls "the cousin party," a wonderful, loud birthday party for six granddaughters and their parents. I heard my phone ring, but because I had dropped it between the seats, I said to myself, "I'll get it later. No time for that now." I finished unloading, went back to the car, and in an afterthought, reminded myself to find the phone. There was a voicemail and one of those horrible transcriptions of the message. I read the first few lines: "Hi, this is Latifah, a nurse at Presbyterian Medical Center here in Charlotte, North Carolina . . . currently taking care of your son, last name Blocker . . ."

The rest was a blur.

Typical for me, I quickly went into high gear, calling the hospital to get a picture of my son's situation. After asking to speak to him through the nurse's phone speaker and praying with him, my brain kicked into planning mode. Do I tell my children and ruin the birthday party, a once-a-year-event? Do I push through the party and then tell them I'm leaving town? As I prepared for the next steps, moving on auto-pilot, my other son and his girlfriend arrived to help with party decorations. Emotions took over and I collapsed into Jake's shoulder, speaking the words I never wanted to hear or say: "Your brother is in the hospital on a ventilator; he almost died but he is stable." Faithful to his precious nature, Jake held me and let me cry and even scream for a moment, but then again, I went into mother-mode. I knew I had to do what I had to do.

My husband and other children arrived with my precious granddaughters, and we had a party.

My daughter, Laura, knew something wasn't right, but she didn't push me. The children noticed nothing except the excitement of the long-awaited party --- a swimming party complete with an obstacle course. After an hour of swimming, I called them out of the water for pizza and gifts. I don't know when I've appreciated that time more than at that moment. I found myself looking around the room at my other children and those beautiful little girls, resting in the bubbling-over joy of family . . . but I knew that as soon as I opened my mouth to share the news, the day would never be the same and my life would change forever. I just didn't know how much.

Looking back and reflecting on that July event, I see my life differently: BANDE and AANDE. Before and after Asher's Near-Death Experience.

Sometimes in life we change by choice. Sometimes we change by necessity because something is forced upon us. And then? Sometimes we change because an experience is so earth-shattering, so destructive, that it attempts to shake our foundations of who we are and what we know for sure . . . it alters the way we view life and the way we respond to crises forevermore. But there are two things that never changed: my faith in God to carry me through the valley, creating beauty from ashes, and my fierce love for my son. Those were not and will never be touched.

So how do we survive these catastrophic events without falling apart or collapsing into a heap of despair? God. Simply God. Everything in scripture tells us to go to Him, lean on Him, and reach out to Him when life throws us curve balls. We are told that "in all things" we can give thanks, and it's true; we may not be thankful "for" the thing, but we can, with God's strength and perspective, be thankful within the moment. We are also told that God's strength is perfect when ours is weak. He knows we won't be able to carry it all, and He is there, waiting to hold our tears and carry us through the worst, which brings me to Psalm 23. In that beautiful passage we read this: "Yea, though I walk through the valley of the shadow of death, I will fear no evil, for Thou art with me." (King James . . . the way I learned it as a child). Notice the words: we walk *through* the valley --- we don't die there --- and we don't have to fear because God is with us. Scripture tells us that He never forsakes us, and because He is the God of every impossibility, we can trust Him to see us through the heart-shattering moments of life.

Do I hope that next year will be less traumatic? You bet I do, and it's already looking up because my son is strong and healthy. But even if next year isn't better and I face the worst, I will put my hand in God's hands, knowing that He is faithful from beginning to end.

Waiting for the Other Shoe to Drop

For a number of years I have called myself a "recovering worrier," but I was a defeated worrier for a very long time. Sometimes my worries involved my job, but most of the time, when fear and worry gripped my heart, it was over my children. About eight years ago, I remember lying in my bed one particular night with worries concerning one of my girls spinning in my head. I was sick and tired of not sleeping and really exhausted with the anxiousness in my spirit. I remember sharing my deepest fear with God, and in that moment, I heard Him speak very clearly to me. It was so matter of fact that I got out of bed, went to my knees, and committed to trusting Him and His plan, no matter what. I also began a serious quest to remove worry and anxiety from my life. I have had an amazing path of victory in this area for these last seven years, but every now and then, when life throws me a series of unexpected, troublesome events, my mind wants to resort back to worry mode. This summer I have faced quite a number of challenges, and earlier this week, I woke up, waiting for the other shoe to drop, so to speak. So what does this say about faith, and what do we need to do when we find ourselves waiting for the next disaster?

Well, scripture is clear. It tells us not to worry. It tells us to cast our cares on God because He cares for us. It tells us that we can have peace that passes earthly understanding. But . . . and there is always a *but* . . . to have this peace of mind and heart, we must be prepared to pray God's Word, fighting back with the Sword of the Spirit, which is the Word of God. We cannot be passive; winning this war requires a proactive and responsive stance to whatever comes our way. Let me explain.

Proactive: I must pray daily, when things are peaceful and when turmoil is everywhere, asking God to keep me in His peace that is not possible without Him. I must ask Jesus to surround me with comfort and calm, no matter might happen in each day. But I must also be **responsive:** when life comes at us quickly and without warning, we must immediately turn to prayer and God's Word. If we respond by wringing our hands and pacing in anxiety, peace will not come, and we can so easily slip into high anxiety, fear, and hopelessness. But it doesn't have to be this way.

Hi, my name is Jean Burden, and I am a recovering worrier. You can be a recovering worrier, too.

I believe deeply that worry and fear are tools of Satan. If he can get us to take our eyes and our hearts away from Christ, then we behave as people who have no faith. And when we show a lack of faith to our families and our world, we look no different than people who live daily without a Savior. Satan seeks to destroy us because when he hurts us, he hurts God's kingdom here on earth. And be aware: he is hungry to devour and destroy you if you love God and are living to serve and glorify the Father.

We cannot pace the floors of life, waiting on the other shoe to drop. We must live in peace, victory and joy, showing the world that life with God, Jesus, and the Holy Spirit is a life like no other. It is a life worth living and worth any sacrifice it entails. Will it be hard some days? Of course! But Jesus told us to be encouraged because He overcame the world, and because of His sacrifice, so shall we.

I visited a dear friend a few days ago, and it was so encouraging to me. She is a wonderful sister in Christ, and she has faced her own reasons to worry in recent days. I have been praying for her as she has for my family and me, and during our brief visit, she reminded me of something that I know but need to hear again and again: Satan has been particularly vicious this summer, trying to take me down, but he is doing it because I have committed to doing anything and everything God asks of me. I have retired from a full-time career for the second time, telling God over and over, "Have Your way with me." So what does this have to do with worry? Well, Satan knows that worrying keeps me from focusing on the plans God has for me . . . plans to use me for His glory. Waiting on the other shoe to drop says that I don't trust God for whatever may come, good or bad. And so, we must wait, but not on another disaster. We must wait on God's guidance, trusting that no matter what we face, He will never desert us and that His strength is made perfect in our weakness. And as if that were not enough, He also promises that He can take every situation and use it for good. So worry? I don't think so. I'm trusting God and I invite you to do the same.

This morning as I went on the porch to pray, I felt the Holy Spirit remind me of a scene from the movie *War Room*. The husband is inches away from adultery, and his wife is at home, praying fervently and loudly against Satan's attack on her marriage and family. Her mentor taught her to use prayer as a weapon, and when she did as she was taught, her husband's heart returned home to her, ready to seek peace and forgiveness. God's response to her prayer to save her marriage shut down the next disaster that was looming, and I believe God needed me to replay that scene in my mind this morning. He needed me to fight back in prayer, not allowing Satan to interfere in my life, my heart, or my mind. And he needs you to do the same.

I beg you today to seek God and His peace, His answers, and His strength. Don't let worry creep into your day, and the only expectation you need is to believe that the next shoe to drop will be a good one, filled with blessings!

Preparation Meets Faith

"Prepare like it depends on you; pray like it depends on God." I have heard this statement many times, and this week it has taken on new meaning.

At the time of this writing, it is September 2018, and in South Carolina we are in the flooding stage following Hurricane Florence. For the moment the rains have stopped, but they will return. No question about it.

Earlier in the week we lost power for about 33 hours. It was muggy and wet and hot, but it could have been so much worse.

You see, I'm married to a man who knows how to do things, and he began Hurricane Florence preparations Monday afternoon, long before the power crashed four days later. He set up a generator and power cords. He tied ceiling fans to deck posts, moved furniture, and put farm equipment in the safest locations possible.

He prepared like it depended on him; I prayed like it depended on God.

I recently finished reading Mark Batterson's *The Circle Maker* for the second time, and so praying circles around my concerns has been in the forefront of my mind. Batterson says that it is an insult to pray small prayers when we have such a big God, and he and his church members have spent quite a bit of time, circling their big dreams, both physically and spiritually. I have prayed these prayer circles before, and I knew that this week was the time to do it again.

As we waited for this very slow-moving storm to arrive, my daughter, Whitney, and her girls and I walked our property. I taught the girls about walking a circle around your concerns and lifting prayers to God, and they were excited to be a part of this walk. In fact, just yesterday, Harper asked if we needed to do it again. ☺ She's right because we do. The storm is over but the dangerous, damaging flooding has just begun.

As we walked and prayed, we asked for God's protection around our home and our children's homes on our Boggy Road property. We asked God to keep the storm from destroying this place, not because material items are so important but because I simply love this place . . .a place I promised God I would use for Him in any way He chooses. A place where I seek God and find Him in the beauty of nature. A place where I never imagined living but now cannot imagine being without. I asked for safety for so many others, too, --- people who had also prepared but needed a touch from Almighty God. When we went inside after this precious time, I was at peace. Complete peace. This is the stuff of God, not man. I love that my husband prepared and I am so grateful for every single thing he did, but my peace came from God alone.

This storm and its aftermath will be gone, and residents and businesses will recover eventually, but I suspect another storm is in the works. Not a physical storm but a spiritual one. If you are in a place of white-picket-fence-perfection right now, I am so thrilled for you. Enjoy it and thank God for it but it won't last. Jesus told us to expect trials and tribulations; He also told us to take heart and stay at peace --- He overcame the world and so can we, as long as we follow Him, allowing Him to own every plan and every inch of our beings. Jesus chose to come to earth, to face a horrendous death that makes our storms look like a rain shower, and He did it all because He loves us. This wasn't easy for Him because He was fully man, fully able to feel the pain of the whip and the torture of the Cross. But He endured it. Why? He knew we could not save ourselves from sin without His sacrifice. He knew we would never survive the storms of life without His life-giving act. He knew we would never overcome without knowing the Overcomer --- the one who calmed the wind and the waves. He continues to calm the wind and waves in our lives, if we will just stay close to Him and allow Him to give us peace when peace seems impossible. Jesus is a miracle worker, and God, the Father, is the God of the impossible.

Peace amidst the storms of life? Completely possible. Just call out His name and surrender your will to His.

And one more thing: sometimes the storms of nature and the storms of life leave us beaten and battered. This past summer was a time of some pretty intense emotional storms in my life. But here's what I know for sure: we can and must praise God, right in the midst of the worst storms. We must praise Him and glorify His name, even when we cannot see the good ending we desired. And like my husband, Dan, we must continue to prepare for the worst case scenario --- prepare through studying God's Word and living in relationship with the Father, Son and Holy Spirit. And when the storms arrive ... and they will ... we can stand strong, knowing that not even a Cat 5 hurricane cannot knock us down or drown us in its floods.

Lessons from Another Valley

There are times in my life when I have asked God for specific things that I needed. Not anything selfish but things I knew had to be within His will. Over and over He has shown me valuable lessons that I want to share because maybe you need to hear them.

First, waiting on God isn't easy but it is vital, and during the waiting, we must be thankful, faithful, and obedient.

Second, when I ask God for a certain thing that I believe is best, He always answers but often in a way that is completely different from what I expected. And of course, true to His nature, it is always *better* than what I expected. When this happens, we must praise Him, thank Him, and be humble before Him, knowing that His omniscience in our lives brings incredible results.

Third, it is hard but urgent that, if we are praying diligently and God closes a door, we trust Him in life's hallway while we are waiting for the right door to open. It often does not happen right away, but I believe it's because God is going ahead of that open door, preparing people and situations to be perfect when it opens wide for us to enter.

Fourth, prayer changes things: sometimes prayers change us because we draw closer to God; being in His presence is transformative. At other times, prayers change our situations, sometimes immediately and sometimes far down the road. Either way, prayer is life-changing. We serve the God of impossible situations, and He is always in charge because He loves us and wants us in relationship with Him. To be in relationship with God, as in any other relationship, we must seek Him, talk to Him and listen to Him --- hence, prayer.

Fifth, God sometimes asks us to do difficult things that separate us from wonderful places and people we love. If He asks, our answer must be "yes." Even when it is inconvenient or seems illogical. He *always* has a plan; we just can't see what He is doing, and so we must be obedient even when it makes no sense. Others will criticize; it's okay. We are only here to please, serve, and glorify our Father. As my son shared years ago: the critics line the stands and throw their comments and taunts, but the one in the bullfighting ring is the only one who knows the battle. As long as we are standing in the ring of God's will, we can withstand anything that comes our way.

Finally, God can and will redeem anything. But . . . and this is a big one . . . we must sometimes get out of His way so He can do what only He, a loving grace-filled Father, can do. This requires trust, and trusting in Him never fails us. Maybe, like me, you need to pray for your situations and envision yourself taking your hands off the problem and putting it into His mighty Hands. Recently I actually wrote my current heartbreak on a slip of paper and nailed it to a Cross; I have given it to Jesus, and I don't want it back.

Did you notice the title of this piece? Lessons from *another* valley. This year, more than in recent years, my life has been a series of very deep valleys and incredibly high mountaintops. At the time of this writing, I had found myself in yet another valley, knowing that the only way out is with God. I have taken His hand, and I am clinging to Him with a holy desperation, praising and thanking Him because I know for sure that He is leading me to better days and places. I suspect some of you are in a deep pit right now, and others will be in one soon, but here's the promise: if we remain with God and place our complete trust in Him, victory *will* come. It might be a long process or a short win, but the end is clear: God always wins, and when we stick with Him, we can remain in peace and joy, despite another valley. That, my friend, is a victory!

Trapped

Until recently we had a ridiculously large young Labrador Retriever-mix named Max. He was a paradox: he looked like a small horse but behaved like a puppy. One evening I was in the house and heard a terrible ruckus in the garage. It frightened me because I thought someone must be out there, trying to break into our home. I opened the door with much trepidation and a pistol in my hand . . . yes, I am married to a card-carrying gun owner. ☺ It wasn't an intruder at all; it was Max. He must have been chasing our kitten, Lila, and when she zipped through the black wrought-iron fish tank stand, he followed her. One big problem, though: she dashed through it and kept going, quickly reaching a safe space; he got stuck. His big body was simply too much for the tank stand, and when he realized he couldn't get out, he began to flail his big frame and the stand against our garage refrigerator. The banging was the ruckus I heard, and I jumped into mom-mode, calming him as best I could and yelling for help. My husband came out, he held Max, and I gently worked his massive shoulders backwards and out of the trap he had unintentionally placed himself within. I had to press against one shoulder, and then he slipped out relatively easily. True to form for Max, he rubbed against us to show his thanks and then did his signature move: he sat on my husband's feet, a place of comfort for him. He was so grateful to have received the help he desperately needed to get out a trap from which he could never escape on his own. And this scenario made me think about us.

Do we put ourselves in impossible traps because we chase things into dangerous territory? Do we find ourselves flailing against impossible situations because we cannot get out without help?

I know that we do. But here's what else I know: Max had owners who rescued him from the trap once he was willing to be still and allow us to help him. God is not exactly our "owner," but he is indeed our Master and Father, and He can and will push gently on our shoulders to release the pressure of the trap and help us to freedom.

So what are these traps into which we run full force? Well, there are traps called addiction . . . traps called sexual immorality . . . traps called emotional eating . . . traps called unforgiveness . . . traps called idolatry. The list goes on and on. We know better but we run into them anyway because there is something we are chasing --- something that is enticing but will never satisfy in the long run. And because these traps are sinful, we can quickly find ourselves caught with no apparent way out. Here's a scenario.

You get angry with something in your church, and you justify staying home instead of attending worship. You fill the day with work-related things to push your business ahead financially, or you fill your day with a string of TV football games or shopping. Whatever the item you find yourself chasing, it's not God. And all of a sudden, you become caught: caught by a passion for something that should never stand in the way of worship. Caught by idolatry. Caught by apathy. Caught by estrangement from the body of Christ. You didn't really plan to go there, but you ran into the idolatry of something other than God, and scripture is clear: *nothing* should come before God. Scripture is also clear that we need to continue meeting together with other like-minded Christians; it's a place to find strength and accountability and yes, a place for corporate worship. Do I understand that sometimes we are disappointed in things that happen in our churches? Of course, but guess what: church is NOT about our happiness, nor is it perfect. Church is about the Trinity: God, Jesus, and the Holy Spirit. It is about worship. Nothing more, nothing less. It is not about getting my feelings hurt or pouting because I didn't get invited to a social with church friends or even about the pastor's sermon. Believing it's about those things makes it about us, and it is NOT about us. It's about Him . . . and only Him. We exist to worship Him, glorify Him, and serve His Kingdom.

This scenario I shared of running toward a dangerous place in only one in a string of many. I'm frustrated with my marriage so I allow a handsome man or woman at work to befriend me, and you know how that can turn out. I am disappointed with my job so I begin to drink or numb my sadness with drugs. Again, you know where that can go. I have been hurt terribly by a dear friend or family member, and I justify unforgiveness and bitterness. Scripture is very clear: these are traps that will come between us and God.

Traps. But God always gives us a way out.

For the past two weeks, we have been "trapped" in our Boggy Road property due to road damage from Hurricane Florence. At the end of week two, workers showed up and repaired the road, giving us access to freedom. God does the same thing.

He shows up every day in His Word, ready to enlighten the path out of the trap. He shows up in the form of God-winks, meant to show us that He is there, waiting to help us. He shows up with conviction --- *not* condemnation --- to make us want to allow Him to push gently on our "shoulders" until we feel the sweet release of freedom from the trap. And then just like Dan and I did for Max, He allows us to stay close to Him, to sit at His feet and find comfort, peace, and forgiveness for our foolishness. We weren't mad at Max for doing something stupid, and God is not mad at us either. He loves us and He wants us to live in freedom from traps we were never meant to enter. I can almost hear Him saying, "Be still and know that I am God" and I will help you find release. In the Old Testament, Isaiah, the prophet, prophesied that Jesus would come to heal the brokenhearted and proclaim liberty to the captives and freedom for the prisoners. When Jesus walked the earth, He read that very passage from the scroll, and then He said: "Today as you listen, this scripture has been fulfilled." Wow. It's like He said, "Hey, guys, remember the prophecy? Well, he was talking me and here I am!"

Our Savior who came to free us from every trap or prison and heal our broken hearts. Jesus. It doesn't get better than this.

If you are in a trap today, even one of your own making, call out to Jesus and the Father. Ask them to show you the way out, and then? Enjoy your freedom and just like Max did with us, sit at the foot of the throne of God. There is no better place to find rest when you have found sweet release!

Putting out the Welcome Mat

As I write today, it is September 2018, and my precious Conway community is in the midst of flooding the likes of which we have never seen before. I tried to explain to some of my granddaughters this morning that they are witnessing a natural disaster that will go down in history, but I'm not sure they understood the magnitude. Water levels of four rivers are higher than at any other point in time, and they are converging on our town, our county, and also in our neighboring state of North Carolina. People's homes and businesses are flooding in unimaginable ways; home and business owners have fought the water with sandbags and even makeshift dams, and some may win the battle, but others will lose everything. They don't *want* the water to come in and ruin the things they cherish so dearly. They are not *welcoming* it in; they are trying to keep it out because they know it is so destructive. And this has made me think about our lives.

Unlike the water that we *don't* want, when and why do we sometimes welcome destructive forces into our homes and lives, knowing they will leave us devastated? Why do we put out the "welcome mat" for dangerous floods of sin?

I believe there are any number of reasons, and they all start with careless sin.

I read and hear daily about men who are addicted to pornography; some of these men are fathers and Christians, so how did this happen? I believe they slowly welcomed it into their computers and their homes, and then this sexual sin became an addiction or at least an evil distraction.

I once had a Christian sister who was one of the most dedicated Bible students I have ever known, and on top of that, she was active in Christian missions. But she also welcomed games of all kinds into her home through her phone and computer, and one day she admitted to me that she was spending hours a day, playing games and wasting her precious time. Games had become an idol. Let me be clear: the games themselves were not sinful, but by welcoming them into every free space of her life, they took over her thoughts and her time, and she put them ahead of her relationship with God.

I had another friend who asked me to cover for her if her husband called me, looking for her. I questioned her and told her that I wouldn't help. As it turns out, she had welcomed another man into her bedroom. Her marriage ended, and she found herself in a custody battle. She didn't lose her child, but she still lost so much by putting this man above her family.

Some people welcome filth into their homes in the form of television and/or movies, while others welcome greed right into their checkbooks. Some welcome and befriend jealousy or anger like it is a renter. All of these choices have one thing in common: when we welcome them into our homes and lives, they seep in, take over, and much like flood waters, leave a mess in their wake.

But God says it doesn't have to be this way.

Years ago I heard a wonderful, visiting pastor say that we must measure every single choice and thought by a plumb line: the plumb line of God's holy Word. And if we do that, we will see clearly that we are welcoming sin right into our living rooms. So what does this measuring line look like?

A woman is tempted toward an extramarital affair, but she turns to God's word. It clearly says we are not to covet things that don't belong to us. That man does NOT belong to her. Remember what happened to David in the Old Testament? He looked at a beautiful, married woman, welcomed her into his palace, and slept with her . . . a woman that not only belonged to another man but one of his own soldiers. Coveting what is not ours gets us into sinful trouble every time.

Another person is considering lying to his boss at work. It doesn't seem like a big deal, and by lying he will find himself in a better financial position. But then he turns to God's word, and the plumb line is clear and straight: Proverbs tells us that lying is an abomination to the Lord, and it also says that it is one of the things that God hates most . . . a lying tongue. Clear answer, isn't it?

I could give you myriad examples but the point is this: we must be discerning about what we welcome into our lives, and anything we invite to live with us must line up with

God's Word and His will for each one of us.

I could try to make this more complicated, but it simply isn't. Seek God's word and His guidance in everything you do, and the welcome mat of your life will be a joy, not a disastrous flood.

Don't Move the Barricade!

"If you see a barricade, DON'T drive around it!" I heard this and saw it on signs many times in the fall of 2018. You see, in our sweet coastal community, we suffered the ravages of Hurricane Florence and its subsequent flooding. For weeks we dealt with tedious, horrific traffic due to closed, flooded road . . . hence, the barricades. Police officers and other officials patrolled those areas to keep frustrated citizens from moving barricades and finding themselves in serious trouble. *Hm* . . . reminds me of God. God's Word is a relevant, living, breathing Word for each one of us, and in many scriptures, we find very clear barricades . . . places where God has erected barriers to keep us away from sin. Let's take a look at some examples.

In Genesis 20, we are told emphatically that we are not to murder, steal, covet or commit adultery. He also told us not to create idols and to honor our parents. Very clear barricades for life that came from God, down the mountain through His servant, Moses. He gave us these commandments to keep us out of trouble --- the trouble of sin. He erected barricades, and moving them should never be a consideration.

But other things are not as clear or straightforward, and we need to consider whether we need an individual barricade that should never be moved. One example might be shopping. Some wonderful people I know seem to have internal self-control, walking away from tempting purchases, while others need a barricade of steel in place. Why? Because for them, shopping is a dangerous addiction, and they find themselves deep in credit card debt. Another example might be eating. Some of us --- me included --- struggle with overeating. God tells us to practice self-control, but really, God? I grew up in a Southern home where mashed potatoes with lots of butter were a comfort food! But even eating needs a barricade when we lose control and use food in unhealthy ways.

Imagine this: you are standing in a driving rainstorm, and you have a huge umbrella. You are staying dry and safe, but then you choose to step out of the umbrella's protective covering. Of course, you get wet; you left your source of protection. This is so similar to life when we choose to move a barricade God has erected, and we find ourselves soaked in sin because we stepped beyond His protective covering.

Sometimes God expects us to stay behind a barricade, not because it is a danger to us, but because someone else for whom this is a problem is looking to us for guidance and direction. The Bible is clear in this, too: we make a deadly mistake when we become a stumbling block for another person because we pushed the boundaries. As Christians we are to be light in a very dark world, and this is a seriously important task.

Finally, God does indeed give us barricades, but unlike the police officers during the flooding, He is not going to patrol us, keeping us from moving beyond the barricades into danger. He gives us free will, and we can use it in any way we decide. But there's a catch: when we choose to exercise our free will in ways that place us directly in danger, sometimes we will find ourselves steeped in consequences that God may allow to stay in place because we have a hard lesson to learn: don't move the barricade!

I pray that as you walk through life, you pay close attention to the barricades God has erected. Let the Holy Spirit speak into your heart to warn you of danger, and seek God's guidance at every turn. He wants to protect you, if only you will let Him.

More Lessons from Yoga

If you hang around with me for any period of time, you will find out that I am a fan of yoga. Two of my children had attended yoga classes quite a bit, so when I retired, I found a class and began learning these challenging and productive practices. I struggle with osteoarthritis, and yoga is the single activity that has made the most difference in my body. In fact, since making this a regular practice, I have rarely seen my chiropractor because yoga keeps my body in line like never before. So why am I telling you about my exercise routine? Well, every time I turn around, the Holy Spirit is nudging me with another spiritual lesson connected to yoga, and here are the latest ones I'll share.

Lesson #1: I attend mixed-gender class with people of all ages, and when I look around the room, I notice some things that I find interesting. Some people are extremely strong and are able to do poses I only dream of doing. One is called "staff pose" and I don't even go there! Others seem to have incredible balance, able to stand in balance poses without ever wavering. Again, not me; I'm getting better, but I still struggle some days to find my center. Still others are like me: very flexible. For an "older lady," I am amazingly flexible, able to stretch my legs way beyond others in class. I especially notice that the men have difficulty with this because their hamstrings appear to be much tighter than mine. Okay, there is a point: just like we all have strengths and weaknesses in yoga, we as Christians have strengths and weaknesses when it comes to the fruit of the Spirit. Remember that passage from Ephesians that challenges us? Let's see . . . there's love, joy, peace, patience, kindness, goodness, faith, gentleness, and self-control. Whew . . . what a list! And as Christians, we are expected to display the fruit of the Spirit in our lives. Now, maybe like me, you realize that you are stronger at some than others. I do really well with love, joy, goodness, and kindness, but that self-control business gives me all kinds of grief. And just like I need to work on my strength in yoga, I also need to study, pray and practice more self-control. Our job is not to compare ourselves with others but to continually allow God to sanctify us through the Holy Spirit as we become more and more like Christ, displaying the fruit He displayed throughout His entire life. Remember: nothing is impossible with God! And there's more.

Lesson #2: After taking a year away from yoga due to my work schedule, I returned and found something amazing: even though I was rusty and not as strong as when I left, I remembered the poses quickly. My instructor says it's because we have muscle memory; I had practiced those poses enough times to seal them into my memory, and when I needed to recall them, my muscles cooperated and the poses came right back to me. God's Word is just like that, except I call it scripture memory. When we read and study His Word on a regular basis, it becomes a part of our memory . . . a part of who we are and how we think. Even if we take some time away from His Word (I don't recommend it!), when we return, it comes right back to us, and aren't we glad? The more we work with the Word, the more easily it becomes second nature to us because our memories place it deep within our hearts and minds. I learned a verse as a child, and maybe you did, too: "I have treasured Your word in my heart, that I may not sin against you." (Psalm 119: 11). So the lesson is this: spend extensive time in the Word. It is how you will begin to know God and change your thinking forever.

Lesson #3: I take my own mat to yoga, and when it was time to return to class after my break, I looked everywhere for the mat, finally finding it in my cedar chest. When I lay down on the mat in class, the smell of cedar was overpowering, and it made me laugh. (Next time I'll find a new storage spot!). But here's what the Holy Spirit impressed on my heart that day: just like my mat smelled like where it had been stored, we often smell like where we've been. And in fact, when we've been living in His Word, attending a Bible-teaching church regularly, and spending time in prayer, we ought to "smell" like it. We ought to be a fragrant offering in a world that doesn't always emit a beautiful aroma. We can take our fragrance of love, peace, joy, kindness, goodness, gentleness, and self-control with us everywhere we go, leaving the places we've been with a better aroma. In the words of a favorite old poem: success is about leaving the world a bit better when we've been somewhere, and I want that to be my fragrant legacy.

Who knew you and I could learn so much from an age-old practice like yoga! Well, I've come to realize that God can use anything He pleases to teach us a lesson. I pray that my lessons are some you needed to hear today, too!

Jean B. Burden

The Paradox of the Old and the New

My husband and I went to Cape Cod a few summers ago, and while there, we took a day trip to Boston. We took in the usual sights, ate some amazing lobster macaroni and cheese, and gorged on a traditional baseball hot dog at a Boston Red Sox baseball game. We did a lot of walking, and at one point I noticed something odd: Boston is a very old, beautiful city with historic buildings and sights at every turn, but right beside some of those revered old places are brand new stores that are quite modern. It seemed like a paradoxical situation to me: how can the old and the new coexist and thrive side by side? Well, in Boston they seem to do it very well, and pondering this paradox made me think about the Bible.

The stories of the Bible are old, all the way back to Genesis and the beginning of time. Every story recounts a piece of God's redemptive love story for His people. From Genesis to Revelation we read of the fall of mankind, God's love for His people, incredible heroes of the faith and the story of our redemption made possible because of God's great love and the sacrifice of Jesus, our Savior. But let's face it . . . it's 2018 and these stories are ancient. How in the world can this ancient narrative work beside our modern lives today? Well, it can, and it does because God's word is timeless. I guess it's a paradox, but one that I am so grateful to know and understand.

If you have never read the Bible beginning to end, I encourage you to do so. Reading passages here and there is wonderful, but walking through God's narrative in the order we find it in the pages of His Word is eye-opening. When I could see how God was in every story and weaving lessons through each one, I realized just how relevant His Word is to us today, even though the stories are ancient. Some people would dismiss the Bible, saying it's old and outdated, but I beg to differ. Look at the story of Esther; we learn about courage and a willingness to do what is right in the face of fear and adversity. Look at Jonah; we see a man who ran from God's calling, and yet God gave him a second chance to fulfill his divine purpose. How many times does that happen today? Look at Paul in the New Testament; we see his complete change of heart and learn about a God who can change lives to do His will, and from Paul's obedience, we learn lessons of perseverance without whining. And then of course, there's Jesus. I would have to write more than can be contained here to share the timeless and urgent lessons to be learned from our Christ, who lived so long ago. Lessons of obedience, love, compassion, forgiveness, kindness, and sacrifice . . . lessons of seeing what people could be, not just who they appear to be, and the list goes on and on. So my point is this: the Bible may be old, and it may seem impossible that we can continue to use it as a guide for our everyday living, but the paradox is true. God's Word is a living, breathing, inerrant documentation of a love story from God to us. It's a manual on how to live in this world in peace, joy and contentment, looking different from the world around us. It's a model of how to become more and more like Christ as we live in the modern world, and it's our path to eternal life.

It's old and it's new. It's dramatic and exciting. It should create reverential fear in us and an outpouring of gratitude from us. It's God's unfathomable gift to us. Don't go to the book store to find the latest self-help book for the problems and challenges of 2018. Go back to the Bible because every single thing you need is right there in its God-breathed pages. Look and you will see!

God's "Omni" Is Everything We Need

As I write the final pages of this manuscript, thoughts of God fill my mind. If you have been reading this book, you know that 2018 has been a tough one for me, and honestly, I'm relieved to be moving steadily toward 2019 and a fresh beginning. But even as I look back, I can see the hand of God everywhere in my life, and three words come to mind: omnipotence, omnipresence, and omniscience.

The Bible teaches us that God is omnipotent. Now, for a language geek like me, word study is exciting and gives me a tingle. (I know I'm a word nerd. ☺) *Omni* is a Latin root that means "all," and potent is a Latin root meaning "power." Makes sense to me: God has *all power*. *All.* How do we see evidence of this in scripture? Well, look at the times when God's people did illogical, impossible feats because God's all-powerful nature was in charge. Take Moses, for instance. God was powerful enough to part the sea, send manna down from heaven to feed His people, and make bushes burn without burning up. And then there's Jonah: our all-powerful God rescued him from the belly of a very large fish. Seems impossible, but God's word says it happened and so it did. Jonah could never have survived this 3-day experience in darkness had God's power not been in charge. And of course there's David, the young shepherd boy who dared to stare down a Philistine giant, returning the giant's taunting with a few carefully chosen words of his own: "You come against me with sword and spear and javelin, but I come against you in the name of the LORD Almighty, the God of the armies of Israel, whom you have defied." (1 Samuel 17: 45). We know the rest of the story, but how was David able to win against the giant? He went against Goliath with confidence in God's omnipotence, not in his own abilities.

And then there's my life and probably yours, too. God has shown His power to save situations that in my mind, seemed hopeless. Only an omnipotent God could do all of these things and more. So I ask you: where is God showing His omnipotence in your life today? Look back over the last year and pay attention to the places and situations in your world that could only be handled by a mighty powerful God. And then? Praise Him and thank Him for giving you strength and power right when you need it most.

But that's not all that characterizes our God. He's also omnipresent. When Moses and the Israelites were in the desert, God was there. When Esther went before the king to save her people, God's hand was all over that ending, even though His name was never mentioned. And in 2018, no matter where I went and what trouble I faced, God was there. I felt His presence in a hospital as I cried in the chapel, and I felt His presence in worship. Even when I could not get a sense of His presence in one situation, I knew He was there because I watched the results of His amazing work. There is not one place we can go to run away from or hide from God, and whether we are calling His name or failing to seek Him, *He* never fails --- He is always with us.

And then there's probably my most cherished trait of all: God is omniscient. Again, let me be a word nerd: omni = all; sci = know --- God is all-knowing, and it's the trait of His that gives me the most peace in my life. I can recount time after time when I could not see the next step of my life or the next piece of a dream, but every single time, when I trusted God to show me in His timing, He did. He always knows exactly where He is taking us because His plan is greater than anything we can imagine or desire. The other delightful thing about his omniscience is that He goes ahead of us so often, preparing details that need to be in place because of what He is about to accomplish. We can't see what He is doing, but in hindsight, we are able to shake our heads in wonder, knowing that He orchestrated every piece to accomplish His purpose. So often I witness Him moving in this way when I finally make up my mind to take my hands off something that I never should have tried to control. When I let go, it's almost as if He says, "Now I can work because I know how this is going to end." God's omniscience . . . I love that I don't have to figure out every detail. I can trust my life to the one who knows everything and according to scripture, works everything out for good.

As you close the pages of this book, I pray that every single message has been one that has touched your heart or will do so in the coming days. I also pray that you will share it with someone else who might need to hear the Holy Spirit-led thoughts of a woman who fails too often but loves God completely. And in closing be reminded: God is all powerful, always present, and all-knowing, and I believe we can trust our lives to Him because He has every puzzle piece in His grasp, and the end result is a stunning picture of His grandeur and glory, shown through our lives when we allow Him to do His best with us. Give Him your whole heart, your whole mind, and first place in all your days, that He might use you for His glory. Be blessed.

An Addendum: Prayer for Teachers and Children

Every year as a new school year is rising over the horizon, my heart and mind become filled with thoughts, prayers, concerns, and great expectations, both for children and teachers. And so I do what comes naturally to me: I pour out my heart in words, knowing that I will use this prayer in the coming days, weeks, months, and years. I share that you might join me in common, collective prayer for all of God's people, but especially those who need our prayers most. I encourage you to use this prayer regularly for the children and teachers in your community.

God, Your children are starting a new school year. Some will come with brand new, expensive clothes, and others will come with whatever they have. I pray that they all feel worthy in the sight of their teachers and their peers.

God, Your children will enter a classroom, some of them entering boldly through the door with confidence, while others step timidly in fear, terrified that they might not measure up. I pray for a hedge of protection around their precious, tender spirits.

God, Your children will walk the halls with friends but also with emotional and physical bullies. I pray again for a hedge of protection, and I also pray that teachers' eyes will be especially attentive to those being belittled by others.

God, Your children will enter the classroom, some with great strengths in reading, writing, and math, and others for whom every single moment is a learning struggle. I pray for the perfect teacher-matches for the children who desperately need an adult with the right skills to help a struggling child.

God, Your children will be on the playground and in the halls; some of them will always be included, but others will feel the pain of ostracism and loneliness. I pray that you give every child someone who seeks him or her as a friend and teachers whose eyes light up when they enter the room. I also pray that the children who do not struggle with finding their niche will have eyes to see those on the fringes and hearts to include them in love.

God, Your children need school supplies and support with reading, homework, and projects. Some will have everything and others will have absolutely nothing. I pray that we all see needs and do something about them. Let our eyes see and our hearts and pocketbooks respond.

God, Your children will be in learning groups in classrooms. Some will be painfully quiet and others will be loud. I pray desperately that the quiet children are not overwhelmed by the vocal ones who always want to be the voice of the classroom. I pray for every child to find his or her voice and not feel crushed by the louder voices; they all need to be heard,

Father, and they need to know that their thoughts and feelings are valued.

God, Your children will enter learning situations, some with no fear and others who are scared to death of failure. I pray, Father, in the words of John Maxwell, that every child will be able to "fail forward" because teachers have created safe environments where failing is a part of learning and growing . . . a safe environment where put downs and ugliness are not accepted. I pray for emotional safety for children to learn their very best.

God, Your children and teachers will enter classrooms with excitement for learning. I pray that their enthusiasm is not crushed by rigid demands and expectations of always coloring within the lines. I pray that they see the value in individualism and in their uniqueness, designed so perfectly by You. I pray that they are allowed to meet every standard with their own creative touch, using their God-given gifts for teaching and learning in myriad ways.

God, Your teachers will enter classrooms to plan for loving and teaching children. I pray that they are valued by their administrators and encouraged to be the very best version of themselves possible.

God, Your teachers will enter school buildings, praying to find a kind, supportive environment for growing as educators. I pray that their energy to teach will never be crushed by cliques and cruelty; I pray that adults set high expectations for themselves of kindness, inclusion, and acceptance, just as they expect those things from children.

God, Your brand new teachers and administrators will enter buildings and classrooms, and they desperately need a minute-by-minute guide. I pray that they see the path You have created for them to walk, and I pray that they are genuinely mentored by others who desire only their success.

And finally, God, I pray for every child and every teacher and administrator who has no advocate. Let us, as Your people, be prayer warriors, intercessors, and advocates for those who need it most. Let us be committed to remembering that not everyone has support at home or in the community, and not all children and adults have the privilege of never wanting for anything. Let us live with them in our hearts and minds, and let our hearts break for what breaks Yours, Father.

Let us love You, love others, pray faithfully, see needs, and do something about what we see. Somebody needs to step up to the plate? Let it be me.

Works Cited

Batterson, Mark. *The Circle Maker.* Grand Rapids, Zondervan Publishing, 2011.

Eldredge, John. *Waking the Dead.* Nashville, Thomas Nelson Inc., 2003.

Gaultney, Barbara Fowler. "My Lord Is Near Me All the Time." Broadman Press, 1960.

Johnson, Linda Lee. "Be Strong in the Lord." Hope Publishing Company, 1979.

Lotz, Anne Graham. *The Daniel Key.* Zondervan, Lea Edition, 2018.

Bible study notes on Jonah. *The Gospel Project*, Volume 5, Lifeway Press, 74-81.

Rushnell, Squire. *When God Winks,* Howard Books. 2007.

Smith, James Bryan. *The Good and Beautiful God: Falling in Love with the God Jesus Knows.* Downers Grove, InterVarsity Press, 2009.

Sterling, Rev. Teresa. Notes from a sermon, The Congregational Church of West Yarmouth, 2017.

Terkeurst, Lysa. *Made to Crave.* Grand Rapids, Zondervan, 2010.

Young, Sarah. *Jesus Calling: Enjoying Peace in His Presence.* Nashville: Thomas Nelson, Inc., 2004.

"War Room." Dir. Alex Kendrick. FaithStep Films, Affirm Films, RedSky Studios, and TriStar Pictures, 2015.

"The Weaver." Anonymous.

Jean B. Burden

Reflections From the Porch

Jean B. Burden

www.ingramcontent.com/pod-product-compliance
Lightning Source LLC
Chambersburg PA
CBHW030523080526
44586CB00011B/305